THE BIORHYTHM BOOK

THE BIORHYTHM BOOK

Plan for the ups and downs in your life

JACYNTHA CRAWLEY

JOURNEY EDITIONS
BOSTON • TOKYO

To *Alice Howard and Linda Morris*

First published in the United States of America in 1996 by Journey Editions,
an imprint of Charles E. Tuttle Co., Inc. of Rutland, Vermont, and Tokyo,
Japan, with editorial offices at 153 Milk Street, Boston, Massachusetts 02109.

ISBN 1-885203-33-0

First edition
10 9 8 7 6 5 4 3 2 1
05 04 03 02 01 00 99 98 97 96

AN EDDISON·SADD EDITION
Edited, designed and produced by
Eddison Sadd Editions Limited
St Chad's House, 148 King's Cross Road
London WC1X 9DH

Phototypeset in Gill Sans and Joanna MT using QuarkXPress on Apple Macintosh
Origination by SX Composing, Rayleigh, England
Printed in Spain by Grafo S.A.

Contents

Introduction

'To every thing there is a season, and a time to every purpose
   under heaven:
A time to be born and a time to die; a time to plant and a
   time to pluck up that which is planted; …
A time to weep and a time to laugh, a time to mourn and a
   time to dance …'

Ecclesiastes 3

There is a time for everything. The human body knows this. It is governed by biorhythms as well as by other regular cycles; among these are those influenced by day and night, the sun and the moon.

Have you ever looked back and thought that you may have made a bad decision? Or that an accident was probably your fault? Or that you caught a cold by not being careful enough of your health? Or began an argument in circumstances you now regret? If so, you have probably concluded that there have been certain days and events which have altered or affected your life, perhaps dramatically, when you might have preferred a different outcome. Thoughts like this suggest the time has come to learn about your biorhythms – the cycles of life within us all, which affect us and our reactions.

The biorhythm wheel, which accompanies this book, makes it easy to follow your Physical, Emotional and Intellectual cycles, and you will find guidelines for interpreting these cycles, while showing how they affect everyday life. There are also hints, information and advice on how to avoid accidents and cope with unsettling times. When you study your biorhythms you can learn to avoid some potentially difficult times.

Biorhythms were first recorded scientifically at the turn of the century, and are likely to remain controversial for some time to come. However, they have many famous adherents, among them Prince Charles. In conjunction with quiet reflection, other healing methods, and as a means of understanding ourselves and others more fully, I believe that biorhythms can contribute to a more rewarding and balanced life.

Biorhythms and me

My father was a Rosicrucian and he tried to teach us about yoga and biorhythms, but few teenagers listen to established wisdom, especially when handed down from parents. My major objection to biorhythms was that the idea sounded too good to be true. However, a 'double caution' day focussed my thinking. On that day I was walking on 'automatic', so could not remember stepping out from behind a bus without looking. I narrowly escaped being run over. The accompanying feeling of unreality, brief loss of short-term memory, or lack of observation, I now know to be characteristic of such double caution days. Later I worked out my chart, laboriously and with complicated calculations – there was no biorhythm wheel available then – and I discovered that my near-accident had occurred on a double caution day.

I became, and still am, an enthusiastic collector of dates of births, deaths, operations and accidents of anyone and everyone. In 1980 I founded The London Biorhythm Company, and developed a simple do-it-yourself kit (and later the biorhythm wheel) to make calculating biorhythms easier. Using this still laborious method, I began to work through biographies and published diaries. Most incidents matched expected biorhythm theory and I gradually became convinced of their validity, as I hope you will too. In the final analysis only you can decide if biorhythms work for you.

Biorhythms and you

Readers have a vital contribution to make to the future of biorhythm studies. All the examples quoted here have been thoroughly researched, mainly from public documents. In addition, the experiences of hundreds of ordinary people have become a valuable part of our research through completed questionnaires relating the exact date of any relevant incident and the date of birth of the person concerned.

It is easy to acquire the habit of thinking about biorhythms. Practise by using The Biorhythm Kit and it will soon become both subconscious and automatic.

The first person to observe and record biorhythms, Dr Wilhelm Fliess, a doctor in Berlin, said that the subject would take 100 years to come into its own. This book celebrates the centenary of his work, 1996 being the 100th anniversary of the discovery of biorhythms.

Dr Wilhelm Fliess was one of the first people to observe and record biorhythms.

Rhythms of life

Biorhythms are three natural, regular cycles within our bodies which affect us physically, emotionally and intellectually. If you are aware of the state of your biorhythms, you can use this knowledge to improve the quality of your life. This brings many benefits. By understanding your biorhythms you can learn to understand yourself. By being aware of your caution days, you can reduce stress, accidents and illness, which helps you to overcome many of life's irritations and frustrations. You can also apply biorhythms to other people. This will then help you to learn to be more tolerant of them.

Your biorhythm cycles begin when you are born, so the first day of life is a triple caution day, a CCC day, numerically 1-1-1. At birth all three cycles begin on the caution line, and rise. CCC days do not happen often; averaged out, there is only one CCC day every seven and a half years, making eight in a biorhythm life.

Biorhythms predispose, they cannot predict. They tell us when we are at a peak, in a trough, or are exceptionally vulnerable. They are internal cycles from within our own bodies, so they can only reflect our potential.

The use we put biorhythms to is entirely due to our own personality and circumstances. When you become attuned to your own biorhythms, you will learn this.

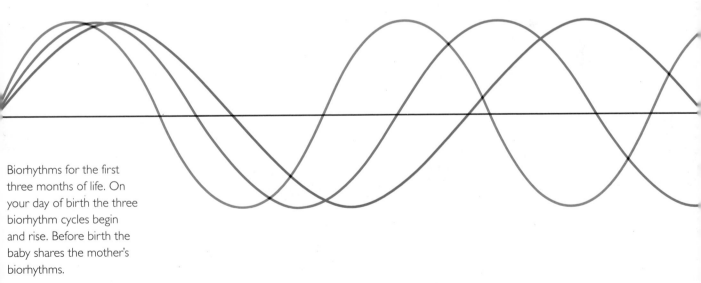

Biorhythms for the first three months of life. On your day of birth the three biorhythm cycles begin and rise. Before birth the baby shares the mother's biorhythms.

What's in a wave?

The three biorhythm cycles are usually depicted as sine 'waves', each taking a fixed time to go from a peak to a trough or a trough to a peak. When a cycle is peaking, those attributes will be enhanced; when in a trough, the body is building up a reserve for the next cycle.

When a cycle crosses the central horizontal line, this is referred to as a caution (or critical) day (*see page 12*). Then we are particularly vulnerable in the respective cycle(s). Statistically, we are up to five times more accident-prone on caution days. If two or (occasionally) three cycles cross the caution line together, the resulting double or triple caution days are additionally unsettling.

The cycles

The three cycles – Physical, Emotional and Intellectual – have been colour-coded by international agreement.

The Physical biorhythm (red)

This cycle is twenty-three days long. It regulates physical strength, energy, endurance, sex drive, confidence, ambition, resistance to and recovery from illness and the efficiency with which the body uses calories. This is generally the dominant cycle in men. Research in the United States in the 1970s established that the origin of this biorhythm cycle is related to the autonomic nervous system (our automatic reactions). Later studies led to the discovery that the Physical biorhythm cycle is also linked to the flow of the hormone melatonin.

A caution day: when any cycle crosses the central (caution) line. Caution days are times for careful and considered action.

Rising caution day: the effects of the caution day will last just for that day.

The best times: when there are highs in two or three cycles, particularly if spread out. Favourable for sporting achievement, high creativity and effective decision making. Two high cycles give balance.

Descending caution day: the effects usually go over two days.

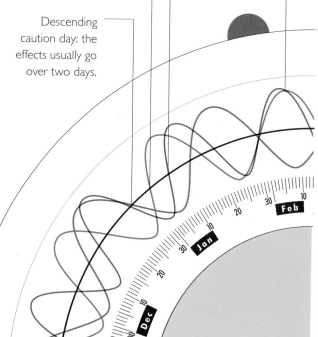

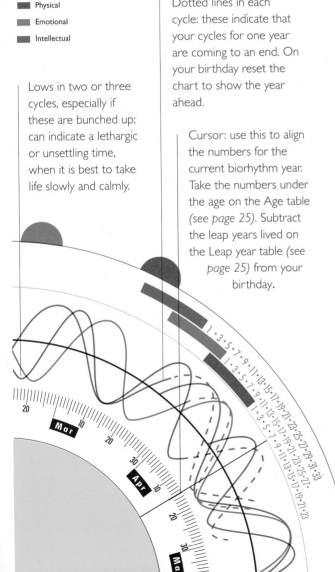

■ Physical
■ Emotional
■ Intellectual

Lows in two or three cycles, especially if these are bunched up: can indicate a lethargic or unsettling time, when it is best to take life slowly and calmly.

Dotted lines in each cycle: these indicate that your cycles for one year are coming to an end. On your birthday reset the chart to show the year ahead.

Cursor: use this to align the numbers for the current biorhythm year. Take the numbers under the age on the Age table *(see page 25)*. Subtract the leap years lived on the Leap year table *(see page 25)* from your birthday.

The Emotional biorhythm (blue)

This cycle is twenty-eight days long. It is associated with the ups and downs of emotions, nervous actions and reactions, sensibilities, sensitivities, creativity, affections, depression and the unconscious mind. In the past it was called the 'Sensitivity' cycle, and has traditionally been observed as the dominant cycle in women and in creative people such as classical musicians, dancers, writers and artists. Researchers have not yet isolated the physiological source of this cycle.

The Intellectual biorhythm (green)

This cycle is thirty-three days long. It governs intelligence, memory, mental alertness, logical thinking, intellectual reactions, intellectual ambitions and, when the cycle is low, intuition. Researchers in Japan believe that this cycle is linked in some way to the secretions of the thyroid and other related glands.

A biorhythm chart

Your chart consists of high days (generally speaking, good), low days (usually of average rating) and caution days (potentially unstable days, when life often appears in control of you rather than you in control of it).

The best overall biorhythm pattern is when any two cycles are high and the other is low for above average buoyancy, with a sense of balance. The exuberance of a triple high can easily annoy others.

11

Caution days

Caution days occur on the first day, and at the middle point of each cycle. It was the observation of caution days in the 1890s that led to the formation of biorhythm theory. Dr Wilhelm Fliess, an eminent medical doctor in Berlin, was one of the first people to record biorhythms (*see page 101*). He did so by noting thousands of caution days. Later he realized that, by counting backwards to the date of birth, cycles could be charted. Caution days, originally called 'critical' days, form the backbone of biorhythm theory.

Caution days occur on the day on which we are born, a triple caution day (CCC) for the baby and, in natural births, usually a caution day for the mother; the day an illness appears or reaches a crisis point; and, often, the day on which natural death occurs. With practice, and through observation, you will probably be able to tell when your friends are having caution days.

Caution days in the three cycles

The caution days in the Physical, Emotional and Intellectual cycles have differing effects on us, depending on the positions of the other biorhythms. There are twenty-seven main biorhythm combinations and these are individually considered (*see pages 26–39*). By understanding their implications, you will be better placed to understand yourself and others. You will also be able to avoid many aggravations and even accidents, and life will run more smoothly with fewer 'if only' regrets.

Physical caution day
- Reactions are noticeably slower.
- There is an increased risk of accidents resulting from over-confidence and risk-taking. Also, there is the possibility of the onset of ailments, varying from the common cold or measles to the flare-up of acute conditions such as appendicitis or heart attacks. For routine surgery avoid, if possible, all caution days, especially Physical caution days. Choose high and rising cycles.
- Natural births tend to occur on Physical caution days.

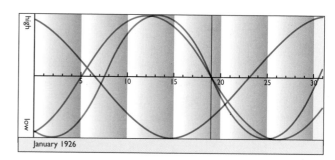

January 1926

Case study: **Harold Abrahams, *19 January 1926***

Harold Abrahams, born 15 December 1899, was an Olympic runner, and the film *Chariots of Fire* followed his early struggles. After his Olympic medal, he broke his leg doing the long jump, never again to race competitively. This was on a Physical and an Emotional caution day, with a low Intellectual cycle.

Emotional caution day

- This is a day when people are very vulnerable on the emotional front. Emotions and nerves are raw.
- Emotional caution days, along with the peaks and troughs of this cycle, always fall on the same day of the week the person was born on. You can study your own reactions to discover your Emotional caution day.
- Labour begins on an Emotional caution day in about fifty per cent of natural births, particularly if the mother has an anxious temperament.

Intellectual caution day

- A day of slow, and often inaccurate, or anxious intellectual responses.
- Try to avoid making important decisions. Relax and wait for better days ahead.
- These caution days are characterized by lack of concentration, absent-mindedness and misjudgements.
- There will be a tendency to intellectual 'stupidity'.
- Mothers over about thirty-four years of age could well give birth on an Intellectual caution day.

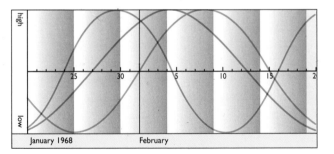

January 1968   February

Case study: **Priscilla Presley, *1 February 1968***

Priscilla Presley, born 24 May 1945, married one of the world's great superstars. She gave birth to Elvis Presley's daughter, Lisa Marie, on 1 February 1968. Natural births frequently occur on an Emotional caution day. Priscilla and Lisa Marie are 100 per cent Emotionally compatible, so they might argue. *(See page 44.)*

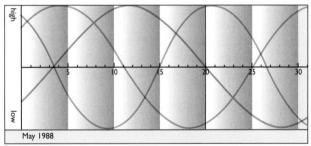

May 1988

Case study: **Peter O'Toole, *20 May 1988***

Actor Peter O'Toole was born on 2 August 1933. He decided to hide his five-year-old son, Lorcan, flouting a United States' court ruling, on 20 May 1988. The high Physical cycle gave him the confidence to take action, but an Intellectual caution day led to an irrational decision which resulted in heavy fines from the court.

13

Double caution days

These days occur when any two biorhythm cycles cut across the central caution line at the same time. The cycles can be heading in the same or in opposite directions. The effects may last for more than one day. There are between nine and eleven double caution days in an average year of biorhythms, or, put another way, less than one a month, but they often bunch up, so this is an approximation.

If the noticeable effects of caution days can be regarded as short, sharp jolts to body, emotions or mind, then double caution days should be thought of as days when your internal wiring is both frayed and short-circuiting. Odd, unrelated messages flash spasmodically around within you. These affect your judgement and perception, and you just do not think clearly.

On double caution days it feels as if you are living through destabilizing, chaotic times, and you probably wonder – Why me? Why now? I am sure we all recognize this feeling that life is on top of us.

However, once you realize that the most probable cause of these upheavals is your biorhythms, it helps put everything in perspective. It is very comforting to know that you are not 'cracking up', and that you will soon enter a better phase. This really is invaluable in getting through a particularly rough patch, especially if you are someone who is prone to depression. Unfortunately, suicide is on the increase. Knowledge of biorhythms can be a useful guide in assisting a carer to help someone when they are particularly vulnerable.

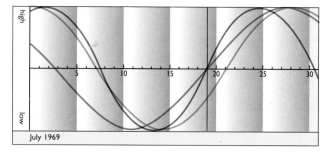

July 1969

Case study: **Senator Edward Kennedy,** *19 July 1969*

Senator Kennedy, born 22 February 1932, has to live with the tragic consequences of the accident at Chappaquiddick, Massachusetts. Early one morning he drove his car off the bridge and a young woman drowned.

His chart is exceptionally interesting. It was a double caution in the Physical and Intellectual cycles with a low Emotional cycle (CLC). The period leading up to 19 July had been a triple low (LLL) phase, which lasted for ten days, the maximum span.

When you wake up on a double caution, or the occasional triple caution, day you will probably not feel much like getting up. This may sound like an old joke, but it certainly is not. It is all too real. Depending on individual temperament, personal circumstances and the caution days involved, you might feel: sluggish, lethargic, slow and liverish, as if you have a hangover;

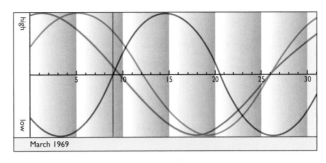

March 1969

insecure or depressed; put-upon and resentful; manic; rather aggressive; or disorientated.

Whatever feelings dominate, these relate to your innermost consciousness. They have been brought to the fore by the lack of inhibition associated with double caution days, and that is one of the reasons we are not too keen to face the day. Deep down we know that we may have difficulty coping with these unleashed insecurities within us.

Even though it may be out of character, as the double caution day wears on we become more and more self-centred. This is a notable feature of double caution days and you can observe this in others. It is harder to observe objectively one's self. We seem to realize that life could spiral out of control, and an apparent survival instinct takes us over. Everything 'I do' on double caution days seems to be in terms of I, I, I, me, me, me. This might help to explain why there are more negative associations correlated with double caution days than positive ones. Something like one-third of double caution day incidents can probably be related to our temporary state of introspection.

We have all experienced one person disrupting a team, or family event, by taking off and 'doing their own thing', or flaring up. Such ego trips are almost certainly connected to a double caution day.

Double caution days fall into one of the following pairs of biorhythm combinations:

HCC LCC   CHC CLC   CCH CCL

Case study: **Jim Morrison, *9 March 1969***

American rock star Morrison, born 8 December 1943, was an unstable person. On 9 March 1969, the singer exposed himself to 12,000 people while performing on stage and was arrested by the Miami police. After this incident, his career never completely recovered. Note, 9 March 1969 was CHC, a double caution day in the Physical and Intellectual cycles, along with a high in the Emotional cycle. On a double caution day the 'double caution' is always dominant over the third cycle. Compare Jim Morrison's chart *(above)* (CHC) with the chart of Senator Kennedy (CLC) *(opposite)*. By their own actions the lives of both were inexorably altered.

[Jim Morrison died in Paris on 3 July 1971 in mysterious circumstances, supposedly a heart attack. His biorhythms for 30 June 1971 were similar to those of people who commit suicide.]

The effects of the two cautions will always over-ride the single biorhythm.

In practice this means that the events associated with each set of these 'pairs' are very similar, and that the position of the third cycle, in these circumstances, has comparatively little importance as its effects lack the intensity to make an impact.

Rising caution days

These days occur when the wave is moving upwards as it goes through the caution day. It is called a rising caution day. The effect of a rising caution day usually covers just that one day, as you are being positively lifted by the upward-moving wave, which is heading towards its peak point in the biorhythm cycle.

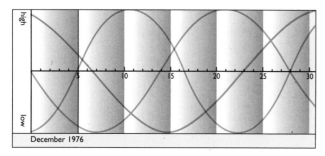

December 1976

Case study: **Dorothy Tutin**, *5 December 1976*

British actress Dorothy Tutin, born 8 April 1930, was helping to raise money for charity on a television show on 5 December 1976. During the show she fell from a camel and fractured a vertebra. She successfully sued the owners of the camel. It was on a caution day in her Physical biorhythm cycle (CLH), a day associated with riding accidents *(see page 87)*, so riders take heed. The wave was ascending so the result was less severe than it might have been, had the cycle been descending.

Descending caution days

In the Physical and Intellectual cycles, descending caution days have effects which usually span two calendar days; in close proximity descending caution days can combine to form a sequence of as many as five consecutive caution days, although this is unusual. More common are sequences of two to four caution days.

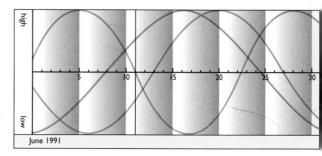

June 1991

Case study: **King Hussein of Jordan**, *11 June 1991*

King Hussein was born on 14 November 1935. He has been king of Jordan since 1952, when he succeeded his father King Talal. On 11 June 1991, he was taken to hospital in Amman with an irregular heartbeat. This was a caution day in his Physical cycle, combined with a low Emotional biorhythm. His Intellectual cycle (will-power) was high and rising (CLH), and, after a rest, King Hussein recovered and was released from hospital with seemingly no ill effects. *(See Heart attacks, page 69.)*

Consecutive caution days

Consecutive caution days occur when two or all three cycles cross the caution line on days which follow immediately one after another. These have a build-up effect. The second day is more noticeable than the first, with the third, fourth and fifth more obviously fraught. This could be a time when life is inexorably altered.

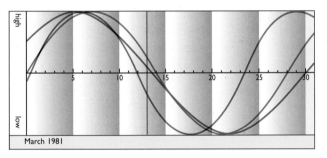

March 1981

Case study: **Richard Johnson**, *13 March 1981*

Richard Johnson, born 30 July 1927, was a leading actor of the Royal Shakespeare Company. In 1981, he was in Hollywood to make a pilot for a new television series. While going out to dinner, he slipped on a patch of oil, broke his nose and lost two front teeth. He had three consecutive caution days: 12 March was a descending Physical caution day with a double-day effect, which carried over to 13 March; the 13th was an Intellectual caution day; the 14th was an Emotional caution day.

Twin caution days

Twin caution days are a double caution day which is immediately preceded or followed by a caution day. This sequence condenses the effects of all three caution days into two calendar days, so there is an extra density to these caution days. Luckily they do not occur often, as this phase is seldom associated with good news.

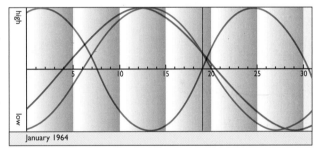

January 1964

Case study: **John Glenn**, *19 January 1964*

Astronaut John Glenn was born on 18 July 1921. In 1962 he became the first American to orbit the earth in a spacecraft. Deeply affected by the death of President John F. Kennedy, John Glenn unexpectedly resigned from the Space programme on 19 January 1964, to run for the Senate in Ohio. It was a caution day in the Physical cycle and 20 January was a double caution day in the Emotional and Intellectual cycles. Due to ill health, he later withdrew from the Senate race.

Characteristics of the biorhythm cycles

Biorhythm cycle	Days in high phase	Days in low phase	Days in caution phase	Days in the mini-caution phase (peaks and troughs)	Number of cycles in a biorhythm life (21,252 days)
Physical cycle (Red) 23 days	2 to 11	14 to 23	Day 1 Days 12 and 13 (**descending** caution days)	Peak: *Day 7 Trough: *Day 19	924 cycles
Emotional cycle (Blue) 28 days	2 to 14	16 to 28	+Day 1 +Day 15	Peak: +Day 8 Trough: +Day 22	759 cycles
Intellectual cycle (Green) 33 days	2 to 16	19 to 33	Day 1 Days 17 and 18 (**descending** caution days)	Peak: *Day 9 Trough: *Day 26	644 cycles

KEY: * means day(s) indicated are the nearest complete day.   + means days always fall on the same day of the week as the person was born on.

A biorhythm life

A biorhythm life lasts for 21,252 days from birth, or fifty-eight years and sixty-three or sixty-four days, depending on the number of leap years lived.

A biorhythm life is calculated by multiplying together the number of days in each of the three biorhythm cycles. In other words: 23 x 28 x 33 = 21,252 days.

A second biorhythm life

At 21,253 days a second biorhythm life begins, starting with the CCC day on 1-1-1. Then the biorhythms begin to repeat their patterns, although the circumstances are different from the first time. A man who has lived 111 years and 105 days has the same chart as when he had lived 53 years and 39 days.

Other cycles

Solar and lunar

Nowhere are the cycles of nature better summed up than in the Book of Ecclesiastes (*see page 6*). Biorhythms are one of many cycles which have a powerful effect on us.

Others include the circadian, the lunar and the seasons, the latter two cycles having external influences. Both our biorhythms and the circadian cycle (partially) are influenced from within us.

The circadian (twenty-four hour) daily cycle

The sun is the most dominant influence in our lives; its gravitational energy holds our planet in place. The electromagnetic radiation from it fosters life on earth and provides our energy supply. The sun sets our overall timekeeping, and the fluctuations of our hormone and mineral levels is evidence of this.

Small clockwork wheels are needed to turn and regulate the movement of larger clockwork wheels. Similarly, the daily fluctuations of hormone and mineral levels move our 'biorhythm clock' on one more day, confirmed by analysis of urine samples, which show the level of minerals and hormones excreted. These can be placed in time-order. The circadian cycle is measured from the low level of activity at around 4 am.

Within the body the hormone melatonin has a cycle length of approximately twenty-five hours. Without the influence of the sun we would probably move towards a twenty-five hour day. Cavers, experimentally deprived of light and outside stimulus, gravitate towards a day length of about 24.8 hours.

The lunar cycle and menstruation

Firstly, it is important to remember that the twenty-eight day long Emotional biorhythm cycle has no direct connection with the menstrual cycle. I have on record three unconnected females who claim to have twenty-three day menstrual cycles. Two of these individuals had serious eating disorders earlier in their lives. This interesting area requires much more study. For some women, menstruation coincides with every third Physical caution day, which occurs every thirty-six or thirty-seven days.

The lunar cycle has an approximate length of 29.4 days. The average number of days between menstrual cycles is twenty-nine days (European women); a number of people have suspected that there is a connection between the lunar and menstrual cycles. This hypothesis dates from the time when the moon was the main source of light after sunset. Before electricity was available the moon had an extremely powerful influence.

People isolated from all other stimuli fall into a waking/sleeping pattern that relates closely to the orbit of the moon around the earth. This suggests that their bodies are influenced by the gravity of the moon. A moon with the power to pull Earth's tides must surely have an effect on us, composed as we are largely of water. A considerable number of people are moon affected. This is stress related.

The playwright Sarah Woods found evidence of a twenty-eight day menstrual cycle in medieval nuns, while she was researching a radio play. Perhaps, and it is a big perhaps, the twenty-eight day cycle might correspond to the menstrual cycle.

I have only been seriously ill once (rushed to hospital at the very bottom of a triple low). After recovering, my periods regulated themselves exactly on the full moon. This lasted for just over a year and then they returned to being apparently random within set limits. I believe there is probably a stress relationship, but that menstruation in general ranges from twenty-eight to thirty-four days. In my case, this meant the first or second day of a period coincided with a caution day in either the Physical or the Emotional cycle.

So, while the two cycles may not be identical, there is some overlap. The menstrual cycle is regulated by the balance of at least five hormones, but research has shown that the hormones secreted by female monkeys are unconnected to any other biological cycle. This, at present, is the research on the subject.

The thirty-six day cycle

Several studies have been done on thirty-six day cycles.

Research over the last decade, at the Royal London Hospital, has revealed a thirty-six day cycle in Crohn's Disease, an inflammatory disease of the gastrointestinal tract. This cycle is independent of the brain.

In the Hersey Railway Study, Dr Rexford B. Hersey, of the Wharton School of Finance and Commerce, University of Pennsylvania, observed cycles of similar length. Dr Rexford spent most of his working life from 1927 to 1954 studying cycles in humans. Up to 5,000 men were monitored over long periods, revealing a thirty-five to thirty-six day cycle. Could there be a connection with the cycle found in Crohn's Disease?

I am convinced that the thirty-six day cycle will be the direction of biorhythm research in the future.

The ten-year cycle

The ten-year cycle is the subject of *The Calendar*, privately published by Dr Caravias-Graas in the 1920s. This ten-year cycle relating to the formative events of each human life is apparently inherent in Mediterannean folklore. It is a cycle I have observed in myself.

Interestingly, ten years to the day after Fliess and Freud quarrelled verbally, Freud found himself in the same hotel lounge and reacted with extreme emotion. (*See Selected reading, Gardner, M.*)

East-West

In Eastern philosophies everything is viewed as cyclic: the seasons and the lives of individuals, including birth and death and the accumulation of wealth and power. Generally speaking, in Eastern philosophies, people see the past as part of an ongoing tradition – a living entity. In the West we see our roots as a subject called history, something that is past, finished, over and done with, and unable to be changed. One consequence of this is that Westerners think of time as travelling in one direction only and that is forwards, like an arrow let loose from the archer's bow. This view provides an historic stumbling block in the way Western peoples adapt to the concept of biorhythms. This difference in outlook is at the root of many cultural misunderstandings, but it shows quite clearly why Japanese and other Eastern-based cultures adapt more easily to the concept of biorhythms than we do in the West.

Do biorhythms really work?

Like many people, you might initially find the uncanny regularity of biorhythms hard to accept. True, no one has yet produced a satisfactory explanation, and for many this regularity can be a major stumbling block. In nature, though, there are many examples of extremely accurate biological clocks. We all know that most plants, insects, fish, birds and animals, and the heavenly bodies,

The famous Prague City Hall astronomical clock, c. 1486.

have totally predictable patterns of cyclic behaviour.

Regular observation of their own biorhythms by people in many countries has confirmed that biorhythms do exist, and are now being viewed as a growing science in which you yourself provide the evidence.

Think of the workings of a clock. The mechanism has small, accurately aligned wheels that set larger wheels in motion as they come into contact. Imagine our bodies are like this clock. Once the time has been set (at birth), the running is both automatic and accurate, although you must expect the occasional breakdown. Of course, some people have a different viewpoint, and look at biorhythms negatively.

For those readers who wish to learn more about other opinions on biorhythms, some articles are listed in Selected reading.

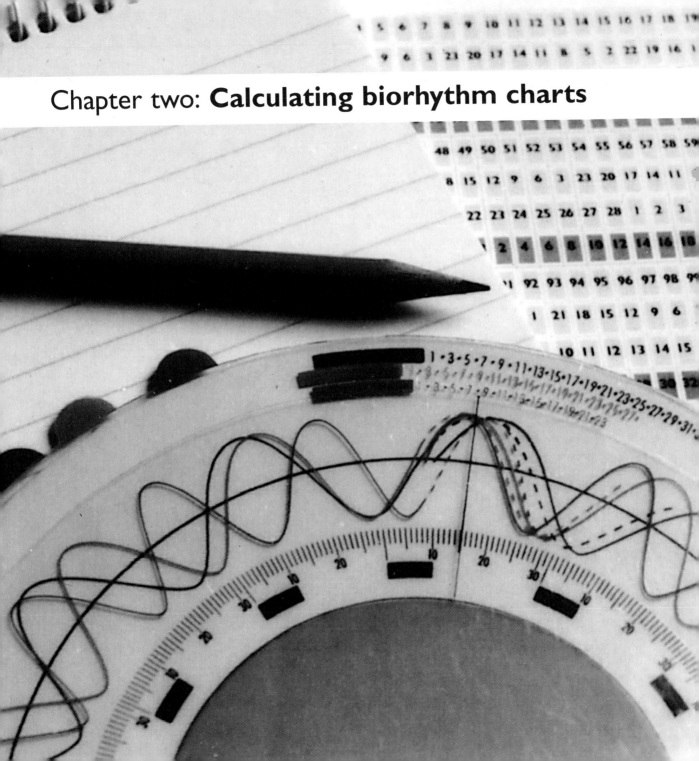

The biorhythm wheel

The biorhythm wheel which is included in *The Biorhythm Kit* is a simple-to-use device for the calculation and display of the three significant biorhythm cycles. It requires a minimum of arithmetic by the user. It will show anyone's biorhythms for any age.

By referring to this on a reasonably regular basis it will help you to understand your own peaks and troughs and your 'caution' days. When you are aware of your own fluctuations, you will notice those of others, and you will become more tolerant.

Remember to always **read the wheel from the centre out,** so that the Physical cycle is read first, followed by the Emotional and Intellectual (PEI).

On the next two pages you will see full instructions on how to use the wheel, with an explanation of the example shown below (*see page* 24). With a little practice, you will soon be following your own biorhythm cycles, which will give you a greater understanding of yourself, and you can also follow the biorhythms of anyone throughout the year.

Part of a display for Paula Yates, born 24 April 1960, for 24 April 1996, set up on 15 April (24 minus 9 leap years).

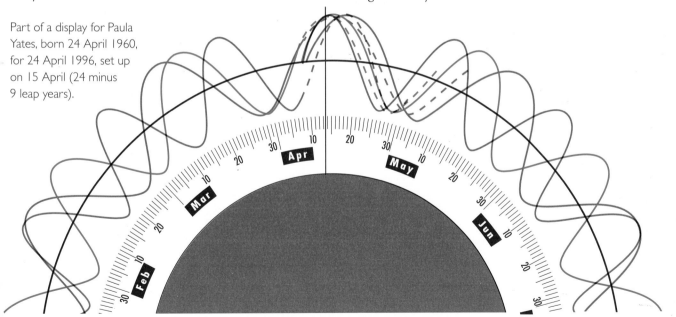

How to use the wheel

To set up the biorhythm display

The biorhythm wheel shows biorhythm patterns for any individual for any year, from birthday to birthday.

• Look for the age you are setting up for in the Age table (*opposite, top*). Sets of numbers given correspond to the three cycles. They are always given in the same order: PHY/EMO/INT (PEI).

• Count the number of leap years between the date of birth and the birthday used. Those born **before** 29 February in a leap year, should include that leap year. (*See table opposite.*)

• Moving the disc for each cycle in turn, place the age numbers one under the other, and over the date of birth. Align with the cursor.

• Moving the cycles as a complete set, now count backwards (anti-clockwise) the number of leap years that have occurred, and place the cursor and numbers over this final date. It must be done accurately.

• The biorhythms for one year are now shown and you can move the cursor independently to highlight any day during the year.

• EXAMPLE (*see wheel on page 23*) British television presenter Paula Yates was born on 24 April 1960. In 1996 she will be thirty-six, and will have lived through nine leap years. To show her biorhythms, take the numbers from the Age table for age thirty-six: PHY 8, EMO 9, INT 7. Set the cursor on the 15 April (nine days before Paula Yates' birthday), and align the numbers directly underneath one another. The wheel is now set up.

Points to note when calculating biorhythms

• Always read the wheel from the centre out; red (PHY), blue (EMO), and green (INT).

• For 29 February (a leap year) in the year you are displaying, the setting works until the end of February (use 1 March setting for 29 February). Turn the settings back one day to get the readings from 1 March.

• At the end of the year, just before your birthday, the cycle lines are dotted to distinguish them from the cycles in solid lines for the rest of the year.

• The Physical cycle always has the greatest impact on any sequence, followed by the Emotional cycle.

• The effects of a descending Physical or a descending Intellectual caution day carry over to the next day.

• The effects of a triple low do not necessarily stop immediately. They may carry over for a day or two.

• Babies born an hour or so before midnight usually take the biorhythms for the following day and although we do not yet know why, it has been assumed that our biorhythms somehow 'lock-into' the next sunrise. Most babies are born between 3 am and 4 am, but if you think you were born just before midnight, for three or four months carefully observe your caution days in the Emotional cycle to check whether they are for your actual date of birth or the following day.

• A six-hour difference due to time-zone alterations between the place of birth and the place of residence could prove important at a very susceptible time. Then, caution days will be one day ahead (or behind).

Age table

AGE IN YEARS	0	1	2	3	4	5	6	7	8	9	10	11	12	13	14	15	16	17	18	19	20	21	22	23	24	25	26	27	28	29	30	31	32	33	34	35	36	37	38	39	40
PHYSICAL	1	21	18	15	12	9	6	3	23	20	17	14	11	8	5	2	22	19	16	13	10	7	4	1	21	18	15	12	9	6	3	23	20	17	14	11	8	5	2	22	19
EMOTIONAL	1	2	3	4	5	6	7	8	9	10	11	12	13	14	15	16	17	18	19	20	21	22	23	24	25	26	27	28	1	2	3	4	5	6	7	8	9	10	11	12	13
INTELLECTUAL	1	3	5	7	9	11	13	15	17	19	21	23	25	27	29	31	33	2	4	6	8	10	12	14	16	18	20	22	24	26	28	30	32	1	3	5	7	9	11	13	15

AGE IN YEARS	41	42	43	44	45	46	47	48	49	50	51	52	53	54	55	56	57	58	59	60	61	62	63	64	65	66	67	68	69	70	71	72	73	74	75	76	77	78	79	80	81
PHYSICAL	16	13	10	7	4	1	21	18	15	12	9	6	3	23	20	17	14	11	8	5	2	22	19	16	13	10	7	4	1	21	18	15	12	9	6	3	23	20	17	14	11
EMOTIONAL	14	15	16	17	18	19	20	21	22	23	24	25	26	27	28	1	2	3	4	5	6	7	8	9	10	11	12	13	14	15	16	17	18	19	20	21	22	23	24	25	26
INTELLECTUAL	17	19	21	23	25	27	29	31	33	2	4	6	8	10	12	14	16	18	20	22	24	26	28	30	32	1	3	5	7	9	11	13	15	17	19	21	23	25	27	29	31

AGE IN YEARS	82	83	84	85	86	87	88	89	90	91	92	93	94	95	96	97	98	99	100	•	•	•	•	•	•	•	•	•	•	•	•	•	•	•	•	•	•	•	•	•	•
PHYSICAL	8	5	2	22	19	16	13	10	7	4	1	21	18	15	12	9	6	3	23	•	•	•	•	•	•	•	•	•	•	•	•	•	•	•	•	•	•	•	•	•	•
EMOTIONAL	27	28	1	2	3	4	5	6	7	8	9	10	11	12	13	14	15	16	17	•	•	•	•	•	•	•	•	•	•	•	•	•	•	•	•	•	•	•	•	•	•
INTELLECTUAL	33	2	4	6	8	10	12	14	16	18	20	22	24	26	28	30	32	1	3	•	•	•	•	•	•	•	•	•	•	•	•	•	•	•	•	•	•	•	•	•	•

Leap year table

1892	1896	1904	1908	1912	1916	1920	1924
1928	1932	1936	1940	1944	1948	1952	1956
1960	1964	1968	1972	1976	1980	1984	1988
1992	1996	2000	2004	2008	2012	2016	2020

Although 1800 and 1900 were not leap years, 2000 is a leap year. A leap year comes at the turn of a century only once in every four centuries. Note that the numbers in the Age table form recognizable patterns.

Check your biorhythms

By being aware of how to use our biorhythms, we can take advantage of our high energy times and appreciate and plan for the restful periods. Remember, for every difficult day, there should be a better one to come. There are twenty-seven major biorhythm combinations and these are given below. Effects vary according to the individual and their circumstances.

HHH

- A triple high is mostly fun for you.
- This is the time to excel in sports. With peak Physical prowess, supported by the high Emotional and Intellectual cycles, many Olympic records have been broken.
- Triple highs can lead to hyperactivity. Do not be too active if you are not used to exercise, or you might regret it later.
- Because you feel so good, you might take on too much responsibility. If you are convinced you are totally right, it could lead to conflict, especially with someone who is having a bad day. Do not be over-assertive or overbearing.
- Early research threw up an interesting sidelight: if you were conceived when your mother was on a triple high, sometimes a double high, there is strong possibility that you would be left-handed or ambidextrous.

Key

Physical
Emotional
Intellectual

HHH

Each letter, 'H' (High), 'C' (Caution) or 'L' (Low), signifies the position of the wave in the cycle in relation to the caution line. Throughout the text the order is always the same: Physical, Emotional, Intellectual.

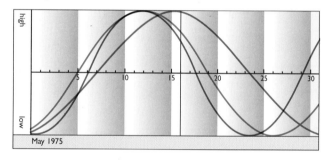

Case study (HHH): **Junko Tabei, *16 May 1975***

Junko Tabei of Japan was born on 22 September 1939. On 16 May 1975 she became the first woman to reach the summit of Mount Everest, accompanied by Ang Tsering of Nepal. Her feat was helped by her triple high biorhythms (HHH), which equates with excellence, particularly in all forms of physical or sporting endeavour. The negative side can be hyperactivity. HHHs are days of supreme confidence when you truly feel as if you are really on top of the world.

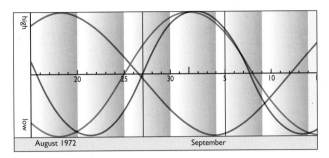

HHL

- This is a nice period. Two high cycles and one low fall into the 'pleasant' category when you are feeling above average, but with a sense of balance. A good day to attain both physical and creative achievement.
- The effects of the two highs easily overcome the low, and this low in particular provides valuable balance.
- You will find creative tasks easier to tackle than those which require calculations. Your intuition is very active.

Case study (HHL): **Mark Spitz, *27 August to 5 September 1972***

The American swimmer Mark Spitz, born 10 February 1950, won seven gold medals at the Munich Olympics, still a record. He was both Physically and Emotionally high over the period when he won four medals in races and three in relay teams. *(See Bobby Hull chart, page 94.)*

HHC

- Your strength, confidence and emotional buoyancy might lead you to make poor decisions today – slow down. Avoid being impulsive and think carefully before you act.
- You might feel argumentative. Think of the consequences before you speak. To others, you will probably appear, however unwittingly, as difficult.

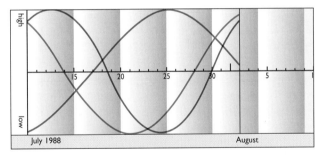

Case study (HHC): **John Naylor, *2 August 1988***

John Naylor, born 15 December 1921, was the astronomer 'Orion' in the *Daily Mail* for over twenty years. His father, R. N. Naylor, founded newspaper astrology in 1930. He died of cancer. The Intellectual caution day is often synonymous with a death from cancer.

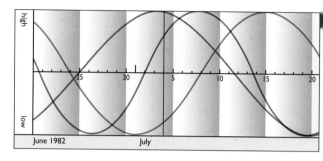

HLH

- This is a pleasant sequence and possibly a highly charged one, with energy and intelligence flowing.
- The two highs will compensate for any low in the emotional reserves. However, you might over-react.
- You could excel in sport, even as a relative beginner.

Case study (HLH): **Freddie Spencer, 4 July 1982**

American motorcycle champion Freddie Spencer was born 21 December 1961. His first Grand Prix win occurred on 4 July 1982. His HLH biorhythms, giving energy and intelligence, meant success in the race.

HLL

- High physical activity is the strong point today.
- With a double low, you may feel slightly below par, and perhaps edgy.
- You are likely to use up a lot of energy to little effect.
- In sports, you might succeed if your opponent's biorhythms are worse than yours, always a good point to remember, but you might still be vulnerable.
- Overall, life should be pleasant if you remember to take things in your stride, and avoid getting upset.

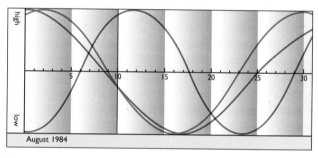

Case study (HLL): **Zola Budd, 10 August 1984**

Zola Budd, born 26 May 1966, was competing in the 3,000 metre Olympic final. Mary Decker was leading the field when she fell under the legs of her rival, Budd. Decker, America's darling, had a reputation for being pushy on the track. Mary Decker's biorhythms (HHL) were good and better than Zola Budd's (HLL). With evenly matched athletes, the Intellectual cycle is important in sport. In this case both Intellectual cycles were low.

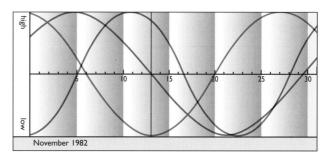

HLC

- This is not a day for thinking effectively, doubly so as you will probably feel slightly down in the dumps.
- You could be absent-minded, forgetful or accident-prone, but should feel reasonably calm, although perhaps somewhat dispirited. Do not rush at things.
- This is not the best of days, but you do have the high confidence to keep you thinking of tomorrow.

Case study (HLC): **Princess Diana, *13 November 1982***

Princess Diana was born on 1 July 1961. At the 1982 Remembrance Day Service at the Royal Albert Hall, London, attendants had been told that the Princess was unwell, and her chair was removed. She then arrived late (Intellectual caution day), by herself, and in tears (low Emotional cycle). She had broken convention and because of the high Physical biorhythm saw it through.

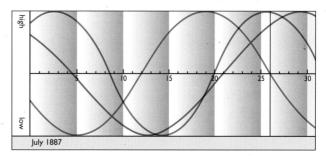

HCH

- Be calm today and everything will go well for you.
- The two highs will make you feel supreme, but you are vulnerable on the Emotional front. Think of the consequences and do not let anyone or anything make you overreact. This might not always be easy.
- Emotional car drivers should avoid over-enthusiasm.

Case study (HCH): **Arthur Croome, *26 July 1887***

Cricketer Arthur Croome was born on 20 February 1866. While fielding at Old Trafford, Manchester, he fell, impaling himself on railings. A spike pierced his throat (which W. G. Grace held together). It was an Emotional caution following a triple high, so he was over-enthusiastic.

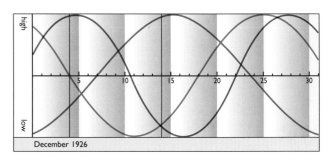

December 1926

HCL

- Have modest aims for what could prove to be a somewhat difficult day.
- There is some physical energy available, so keep busy on routine matters or jobs that require little thought.
- Do not get into rows. Bite your tongue before you say anything you might later regret. Irritability or loss of temper is a strong possibility.
- This sequence, with the high Physical cycle and caution in the Emotional, is often associated with birth.

Case study (HCL): **Agatha Christie, *4 December 1926***

Author Agatha Christie was born on 15 September 1890. Already famous in 1926, she disappeared on an Emotional caution day (HCL). It seems that she suffered an emotional breakdown. She also had a high Physical cycle which gave her the confidence to take action, and her Intellectual cycle was low, leaving her judgement poor. She was found safe and well in a hotel on 14 December (LLH).

HCC

- This could be an unsettling day, for you have lots of energy, but no direction.
- This is a day of internal conflicts at every level.
- Take care and think of the more relaxed and less pressured days to come.

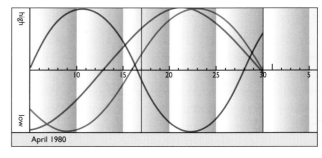

April 1980

Case study (HCC): **Tom McMillan, *17, 30 April 1980***

Tom McMillan, the MP for Glasgow, was born on 12 February 1919. In wet conditions he slipped and fell off a bus on 17 April 1980 (CHH). In hospital he remained unconscious until his death on 30 April (HCC).

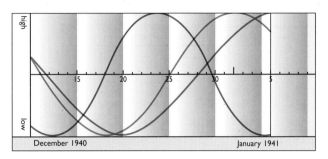

LHH

- A pleasant day and a good one for you to be creative and to make decisions.
- Do not try to work too hard.
- Your energy reserves are low and you might become tired more quickly than usual.

Case study (LHH): **Amy Johnson, *5 January 1941***

Amy Johnson, born 1 July 1903, was England's foremost pioneer aviatrix. She broke several records, including flying from the UK to Australia in nineteen days, the first woman to fly a plane there. In 1941 her plane disappeared over the Thames Estuary. Her body was never recovered. Her biorhythms were balanced (LHH), telling us that the tragedy was probably mechanical failure. It was wartime. Was her plane accidentally shot down?

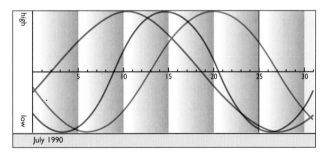

LHL

- A generally unremarkable phase but emotional buoyancy could lead to trouble.
- Left to your own devices you could be creative or exceptionally intuitive.
- Try not to overdo things physically. Ideally you should aim for peace and quiet during this phase. This is not a time for overwork or pushing yourself too far.

Case study (LHL): **Mary Flynn, *25 July 1990***

Housewife Mary Flynn was born on 18 March 1949. Her gossip upset a female acquaintance who then assaulted her. Mary's biorhythms were LHL. High Emotion and low Intellect made her somewhat volatile.

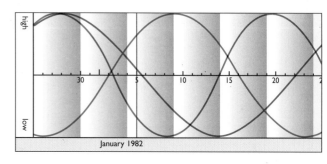

January 1982

LHC

- It might be difficult to make good decisions today. If you can, try to postpone any crucial decisions, especially if these have emotional overtones.
- With low energy and an Intellectual caution day, take care around the house. If driving long distances, plan for adequate rest stops before you set off.

Case study (LHC): **Anna Ford, *5 January 1982***

English newsreader Anna Ford, born 2 October 1943, went into labour on an Intellectual caution day. Later she gave birth to her daughter, Clare. This sub- pattern for birth often applies to mothers over the age of about thirty-four. This observation was one of the first recorded by The London Biorhythm Company.

LLH

- You will not feel like doing much today, and even intellectual efforts themselves will be hard won.
- As this is likely to be a lethargic phase for you, there is a strong possibility that sitting for long periods when you are both emotionally and physically drained could make you drowsy. Two cycles are running at low ebb.
- Two lows will make you feel insecure and you will worry about this because your intellect is high.

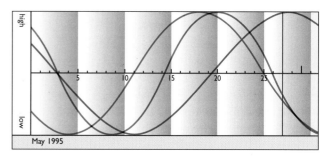

May 1995

Case study (LLH): **Christopher Reeve, *27 May 1995***

Superman star Christopher Reeve, born 25 September 1952, was wearing a helmet when his horse refused a jump. He fell and broke his neck (LLH). The Emotional and Physical biorhythm cycles were descending. He had had an Emotional caution day two days before the accident and a Physical caution day only one day before.

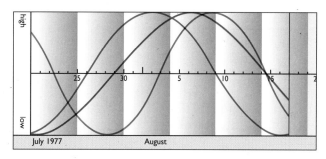

Case study (LLL): **Elvis Presley, *17 August 1977***

Elvis Presley was born on 8 January 1935. The first official cause of Elvis' death was a heart attack. This was later discounted, although a non-fatal heart attack was quite possible on 17 August (LLL). The revised version was death from a drugs build-up or overdose. Compare Elvis' chart to that of Jimi Hendrix (see *page 76*).

LLL

- Do not ignore this phase. Take extra rest and relax.
- You feel like a zombie. Knowing why you are in this exhausted state has a cushioning effect, removing some worry and stress. Plan ahead for the eventual upturn.
- People who die peacefully in their sleep usually have this pattern, especially elderly people whose death cannot be attributed to any one cause.

LLC

- You will make stupid decisions, ones you later regret.
- The desire for freedom, to cut loose from the past and begin again, can dominate your thoughts. However, this desire is seldom combined with any sense of future direction. It results from accumulated tensions. Once these tensions are released you rarely look back. Do not let this safety valve explode until you have made plans for the future.
- This is not a common sequence.

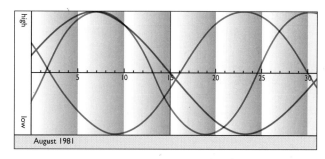

Case study (LLC): **Mr Anonymous, *15 August 1981***

In a fraud investigation, one of those involved, born 26 September 1926, made a casual error on an Intellectual caution day. He sent in an official signed document on which, in haste, he had written the number of a separate registered company. Ten years later the partially erased number provided a crucial clue in the jigsaw.

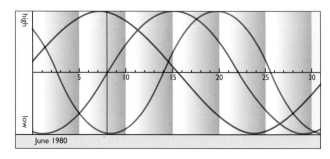

June 1980

LCH

- A 'so-so' day. Make use of the high Intellectual cycle. Try not to snap at others; you could over-react.
- There is an excess of nervous energy and you probably feel emotional and insecure. Your thoughts might be random or over-active.
- You could experience the accumulative effects of tiredness, emotional confusion, and yet feel the need to look clever. 'One-upmanship' is the key word today. You might have a sneery attitude or be verbally aggressive.

Case study (LCH): **Henry Kissinger,** *8 June 1980*

Henry Kissinger was born on 25 May 1923. The former US Secretary of State and Nobel Laureate for Peace slightly injured his head when he fell from his speaking platform in Illinois. He was treated briefly in hospital, but was later released with no ill effects.

Another example of an incident on an LCH day is the housewife who fell from a ladder tipping paint on the floor, but not injuring herself. The Emotional caution, and low Physical, meant both were over-enthusiastic. *(See Ratner chart, page 71.)*

LCL

- This day can be associated with actions, which you are aware overstep the norms of behaviour. On one level you realize this, yet you are unable to pull yourself back from the brink. Later, of course, you usually have regrets. You might brood, grow resentful or become spiteful – perhaps even develop an obsession.
- Low Physical and low Intellectual biorhythm cycles, together with an Emotional caution day, can result in feelings of paranoia, if the predisposition is already within one's personality.
- Behaviour might be disruptive.

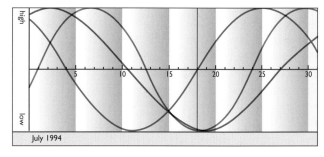

July 1994

Case study (LCL): **Bronwyn Bishop,** *18 July 1994*

Australian Senator Bronwyn Bishop, born on 19 October 1942, became 'a bit cross'

and allegedly tried to enter the cockpit on a delayed flight – typical LCL day behaviour?

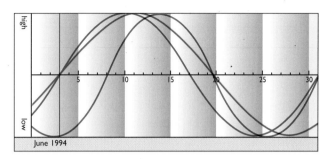

June 1994

LCC

- This is likely to be a traumatic day. Luckily LCC days do not happen very often. That is the good news.
- You may feel that you are misplaced in time or space, so this is definitely a day to avoid climbing ladders. Falls from ladders, especially by men, occur frequently and often with life-long consequences. Such incidents account for the highest number of accidents in our files after car accidents. Most of these falls could have been avoided with due care.
- This pattern is also discussed under suicides.

Case study (LCC): **Wenda Kapteyn,** *3 June 1994*

Dutch Wenda Kapteyn was born on 12 December 1953. She was working on a ladder when someone came along and they began to chat. She stepped backwards off the ladder, fell and was seriously injured. She is now a paraplegic. It was a caution day in the Emotional biorhythm, so she was feeling lonely and bored and wanted to talk. It was an Intellectual caution day, so she was not alert or thinking clearly, and the Physical cycle was low.

CHH

- Over-confidence in your own abilities could mean a physical accident today – do not rush around or take risks. These are today's key words.
- You feel buoyant emotionally and intellectually.
- A good day for a job interview; you should come across well, and the Physical caution day might prevent you from appearing domineering. This day should give you an excellent start to anything creative.
- If you are driving or riding, be especially careful not to take risks. Remember 'road rage'/aggression.

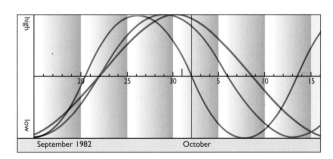

September 1982   October

Case study (CHH): **Larry Martin,** *2 October 1982*

Martin, born 14 May 1952, was in a car accident on 2 October 1982. He suffered a severe blow to the back. He has had back surgery twice, but is still in chronic pain.

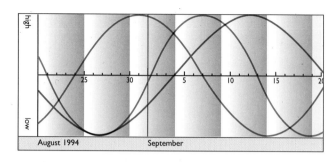

CHL

- You may feel that you have no internal balance. Allow extra time and double-check everything. You could oversleep, thus starting the day badly. There is the likelihood of oversleeping on Physical caution days.
- The high Emotional cycle gives a spark of optimism.
- On a caution day in the Physical cycle, reactions are six times slower than in a high phase. This is not a frequent sequence.

Case study (CHL): **Dingiri Banda Wijetunge, *1 September 1994***

President Dingiri Banda Wijetunge was born on 15 February 1922. He was elected President of Sri Lanka in May 1993. He was admitted to hospital with fatigue on 1 September 1994 (CHL). The President soon recovered. It was a Physical caution day, but the cycle was rising. Although he was intellectually exhausted, his biorhythms were adequate and saw him through.

CHC

- Make allowances for yourself – you will almost certainly be clumsy and forgetful. Allow extra time for everything you do.
- Aggression may come to the surface, due to the Physical caution day. Plots and confrontations may be planned and enacted, due to the combined effects of the Physical and Intellectual cautions, but they are undoubtedly doomed.
- You feel unsteady and insecure.
- Elderly people often fall, or fall out of bed on this day. Carers take note.

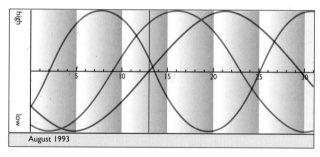

Case study (CHC): **Hilda Norton, *13 August 1993***

Elderly widow Hilda Norton was born on 17 June 1901. On 13 August 1993 (CHC) she fell from bed, was not badly hurt, but taken to hospital. This happens to the elderly because they misjudge the distance to the floor.

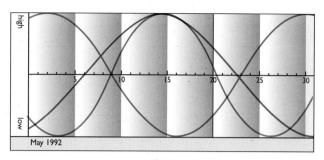

May 1992

CLH

- Your Intellectual high might not see you through today. Take extra care with coordination.
- This is an odd time: you may have a crisis of confidence and feel confused and unstable due to the low Emotional cycle and the Physical caution day.
- You are buoyed up by the high Intellectual phase.
- On average, these are days when life is pulling you in all directions.

Case study (CLH): **Simon Burns, *20 May 1992***

British MP Simon Burns was born on 6 September 1952. Outside the Houses of Parliament, he was walking towards his car and took a short-cut. He had to jump a 46-centimetre (18-inch) link fence in Dean's Yard, when he caught his foot, and fell in front of gaping tourists. He had a big gash in one knee. *(See Tutin chart, page 16.)*

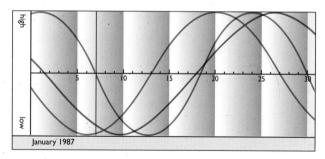

January 1987

CLL

- You may feel a tug of war going on between conflicting stresses – do not expect a smooth ride today.
- Tomorrow you will feel better, so do not let today get you down. Those of a volatile temperament should resist the temptation to go on the rampage.
- This is a day when self-confidence can be shattered. If you are basically docile, the caution Physical cycle, together with the low Intellectual cycle, could make you feel it is easier to give in for the sake of peace and quiet. Coping with the lack of self-confidence when you feel stressed is not easy.

Case study (CLL): **Prince Edward, *7 January 1987***

Prince Edward, born on 10 March 1964, had completed some training with the Royal Marines, when he suddenly quit. He was on a Physical caution day with lows in his other cycles. Prince Edward made a temperamental decision, probably in the face of parental pressure.

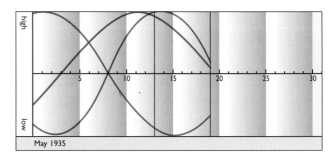

May 1935

CLC

- With poor reactions and slow intellectual skills today, do not take any chances.
- You may experience a crisis in confidence combined with extreme slowness in reactions, perhaps even a complete failure to grasp reality.
- Sequence linked to heart attacks and strokes.

Case study (CLC): **'Lawrence of Arabia'**, *19 May 1935*

T. E. Lawrence, the legendary 'Lawrence of Arabia', was born on 15 August 1888. In Dorset, while riding his motorcycle on 13 May 1935, he swerved to avoid two boys riding bicycles abreast around a sharp corner. It was an HLH day. He died from his injuries on 19 May, which was a CLC day. The accident was not his fault.

CCH

- An Intellectual high is your main asset today. You could be accident-prone, nevertheless, and you could easily over-react to situations.
- You may have a crisis in confidence.
- Extreme slowness in reactions, which may be distorted; perhaps even a complete failure to grasp reality.
- You have too much energy from the caution days in the Physical and Emotional cycles.
- Very similar to a CCL day.
- This sequence is linked to heart attacks and strokes.
- Births and deaths can be correlated with this sequence.

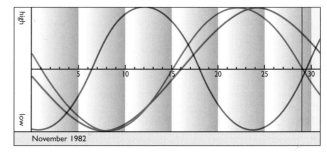

November 1982

Case study (CCH): **Prince Claus**, *29 November 1982*

Prince Claus of The Netherlands, the husband of Queen Beatrix, was born on 6 September 1926. On 29 November 1982, he returned unexpectedly to the Swiss clinic which had treated him for depression in October 1982. The Physical and Emotional caution day is associated with Brief Recurrent Depression.

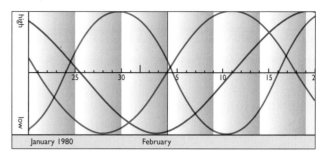

January 1980   February

CCL

- Not a particularly wonderful time.
- You may have no balance whatsoever, so little will go right for you today. Try not to get rattled about it. Take life slowly and 'as it comes'. Confidence is haywire.
- You may experience slow and distorted reactions and have an abundance of nervous energy.
- You may be foul-tempered, rather than moody.
- You could be accident-prone. Avoid using ladders. A day strongly associated with industrial accidents.
- Births and deaths can be correlated with this pattern.

Case study (CCL): **David Wilkie,** *4 February 1980*

British swimmer David Wilkie, born 8 March 1954, broke his nose and his left hand in a car crash on 4 February 1980. The caution day in the Physical and Emotional cycles with a low Intellectual cycle meant that he was particularly accident prone on this day. By the next day, 5 February 1980, the Emotional cycle was in a high and he struggled to attend an Olympic fund-raising event in Gloucester despite his injuries.

CCC

- Triple caution days come once in seven to nine years. Take care.
- All logic would suggest that CCC is likely to be a doom-laden day and that you would be better off not getting up. It just is not like that and I have no idea why. In all the research I have done, I have found only two examples of any incident related to a triple caution day, perhaps because there are very few of these days in a lifetime. Time and research will provide the answer.

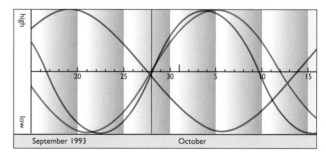

September 1993   October

Case study (CCC): **Ronnie Kray,** *28 September 1993*

London gangster Ronnie Kray was born on 17 October 1933. He had a heart attack in prison on a triple caution day, a likely day for a heart attack. [He died in 1995.]

39

Using the wheel to check compatibility

Compatibility is an amusing aspect of the study of biorhythms, although as yet unproven. Two people are said to be biorhythmically compatible when their biorhythms are similar. Twins are the most extreme examples of this. Generally, people are compatible with others with whom they are most biorhythmically similar. To calculate exactly how biorhythmically compatible two people are follow these simple steps:

1. Set up the biorhythms of the **older** person for the year in which the **younger** person was born. For example, if the older person is five when the younger person was born, then align the figures in the Age table (*see page 25*) for age 5 with the older person's date of birth. Then count back the number of leap years between the two birth dates.

2. Move the cursor to pinpoint the date of birth of the younger person.

3. Use the cursor to count the number of days after but not including the date of birth of the younger person (as displayed on the chart just set up) up to, and including, the first **rising** caution day following this. Do this for each cycle in turn: then refer to the Compatibility table(*see right*).

Note: Caution days are the days when any cycle crosses the central division. A rising caution day is one where the biorhythm is travelling **upwards** at the time it crosses the central line.

Key for Compatibility table: *Physical: 0% would actually fall on day 11.5. **Intellectual: 0% would actually fall on day 16.5.

Compatibility table

Days between the Biorhythm Cycles	Physical Cycle	Emotional Cycle	Intellectual Cycle
0	100%	100%	100%
1	91%	93%	94%
2	83%	86%	88%
3	74%	79%	82%
4	65%	71%	76%
5	56%	64%	70%
6	48%	57%	64%
7	39%	50%	58%
8	30%	43%	52%
9	22%	36%	46%
10	13%	29%	39%
11	4%	21%	33%
12	0% *	14%	27%
13	13%	7%	21%
14	22%	0%	15%
15	30%	7%	9%
16	39%	14%	3%
17	48%	21%	0% **
18	56%	29%	9%
19	65%	36%	15%
20	74%	43%	21%
21	83%	50%	27%
22	91%	57%	33%
23	100%	64%	39%
24		71%	46%
25		79%	52%
26		86%	58%
27		93%	64%
28		100%	70%
29			76%
30			82%
31			88%
32			94%
33			100%

In partnerships and marriage

Incompatibility

Biorhythm compatibility is fixed on the date of birth of the **younger** of the two people and does not vary numerically. It is a convenient way of expressing the number of days any two people's biorhythms are apart in each of the three cycles.

EXAMPLE: Set up Prince Charles' (the **older** person) biorhythms for the day Princess Diana (the **younger** person) was born.

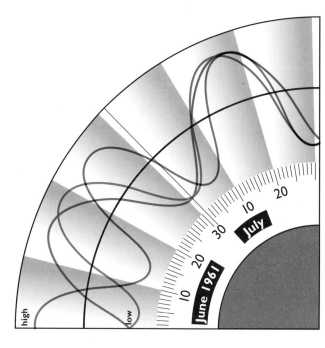

Princess Diana and Prince Charles on the balcony of Buckingham Palace. The Princess was pregnant at the time.

Case study: **Prince Charles on Princess Diana's birthday, 1 July 1961**

Prince Charles, born 14 November 1948, and Princess Diana, born 1 July 1961, have somewhat incompatible biorhythms. As the elder, the Prince's chart illustrated here shows his biorhythms at the time of his future wife's birth on 1 July 1961. Their compatibility is: Physical 4 per cent, Emotional 43 per cent, and Intellectual 52 per cent.

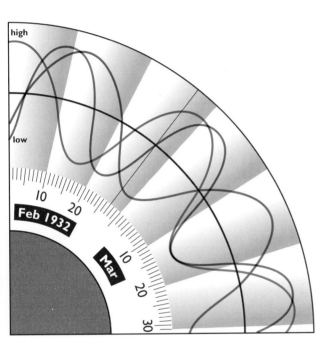

Case study: **Richard Burton on Elizabeth Taylor's birthday, *27 February 1932***

Richard Burton, born 10 November 1925, and Elizabeth Taylor, born 27 February 1932, were extremely compatible in the Physical biorhythm – 100 per cent. The Emotional cycle was good at 71 per cent, but the Intellectual cycle was lowish at 39 per cent. They married twice and divorced twice.

Extremes of compatibility

Try to avoid the extremes of compatibility, that is both very high and very low. High compatibility can be exciting but short-lived, while low is probably a non-starter anyway.

Couples who divorce, and remarry each other, generally have a very high Physical biorhythm compatibility (100 per cent or 91 per cent), resulting in rivalry and dramatic fights. They are usually low in the other cycles. Remarriage after divorce happens more often than is generally realized.

Elizabeth Taylor and Richard Burton on the set of *Who's afraid of Virginia Woolf* in 1966.

Couples compatible in one cycle only

In many marriages, the couple turns out to be compatible in only one cycle. While the marriage may survive, it may not be wholly satisfying to either partner.

Couples with 100 or 93 per cent Emotional compatibility often have enormous rows, particularly if both parties are 'hot-headed'. The good times may be enjoyable, but any argument is likely to be horrendous and intended to wound. It is a struggle for emotional dominance between two evenly matched opponents.

I have friends who are 100 per cent Emotionally and Intellectually compatible. Their Physical compatibility is low. At first no happier couple could be found. Then the arguments began and became more frequent. They married and divorced within a year.

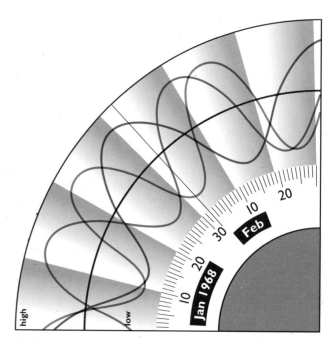

Michael Jackson and Lisa Marie in Hungary.

Case study: **Michael Jackson on Lisa Marie Presley's birthday, 1 February 1968**

Superstar Jackson, born 29 August 1958, married Lisa Marie Presley, born 1 February 1968. They are very compatible in one cycle only, the Emotional, 93 per cent, and have fairly low compatibility in the other two cycles: 39 per cent Physical, and 33 per cent Intellectual. This suggests that one will try to dominate.

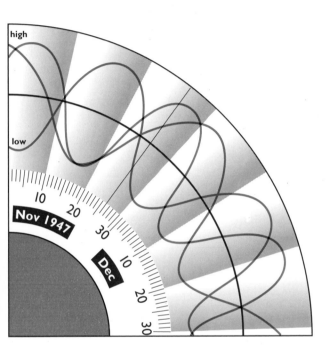

Case study: **President Bill Clinton on Hillary Rodham Clinton's birthday, 26 November 1947**

President Clinton was born on 19 August 1946 and Hillary on 26 November 1947. The couple are 65 per cent Physically compatible, 14 per cent Emotionally compatible and 88 per cent Intellectually compatible. The low Emotional biorhythm means that it is likely they argue a lot, but Intellectually they pull together.

Couples compatible in two cycles

Many couples fall into this category of reasonable compatibility. They are compatible, usually avoiding the extremes of biorhythm compatibility. They work fairly well together and life is satisfying enough for them to get along successfully.

Biorhythm compatibility may not be straightforward, and other factors could have an equally strong influence. Until we get to know someone, perhaps until we live with them, we all tend to be on our best behaviour.

First Lady Hillary Rodham Clinton adjusts her husband's collar at the 10th anniversary conference of the Democratic Leadership Council in 1994.

Couples with the best compatibility

The people I have known who seem totally right for each other over a long period have all had biorhythms that are over 50 per cent compatible in all three cycles.

A Royal husband and wife, King Juan Carlos and Queen Sophia of Spain, attend a wedding.

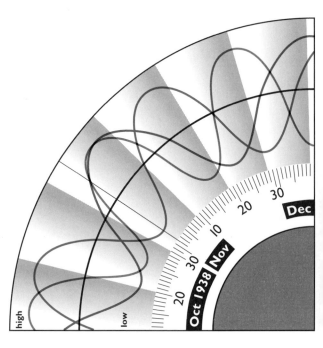

Case Study: **King Juan Carlos on Queen Sophia's birthday,** *2 November 1938*

King Juan Carlos of Spain was born on 5 January 1938. Queen Sophia was born on 2 November 1938. They have been married for more than thirty years. They have good overall compatibility: 83 per cent in the Physical cycle, 50 per cent in the Emotional cycle and 76 per cent in the Intellectual cycle.

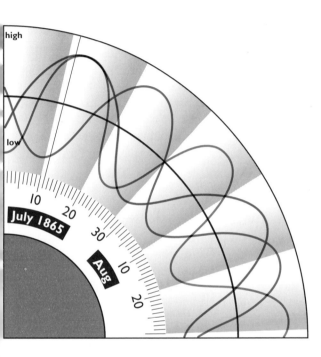

Couples with excellent compatibility

The best basis for a marriage biorhythmically speaking is for all three cycles to be just over 50 per cent. This is shown in the example here where James and Sarah Burgess were married for 82 years.

A traditional wedding photograph from the late nineteenth century, a time when marriages were expected to last a lifetime.

Case study: **James Burgess on Sarah Gregory Burgess' birthday, 11 July 1865**

James Burgess, born 3 March 1861, and Sarah Gregory Burgess, born 11 July 1865, hold the record as the longest married British couple, celebrating their 82nd wedding anniversary in 1965. Their excellent biorhythm compatibility was: Physical 65 per cent, Emotional 64 per cent, Intellectual 58 per cent.

Family relationships

There is considerable evidence that the 'favourite' child (the one a parent gets along with best) is the one with whom the parent is most biorhythmically compatible. Try this for yourself – and be truthful. The principle will work just as well for other family relationships.

The reaction of the mother to the child may depend on whether the mother's biorhythms were going up or down at the time of birth. There could also be a relationship between post-natal depression and the biorhythm position of the mother at the time of birth.

The biorhythm compatibility within the family of Nobel Laureate Marie Curie was good. Both parents and children led fulfilling lives. Madame Curie was one of the first two women in Europe to gain a doctorate and became the first woman professor at the Sorbonne in Paris. She is most famous for winning two Nobel Prizes, one with her husband Pierre. Daughter Irene became a physicist, also winning a Nobel Prize with her husband, Frederic Joliot. Younger daughter Eve became a well known concert pianist and her mother's biographer.

Biorhythm compatibility in a family must be considered alongside individual interests and other achievements.

Within the Curie family the Intellectual cycle is dominant. However, in a family of artists, the Emotional biorhythm would be the dominant one.

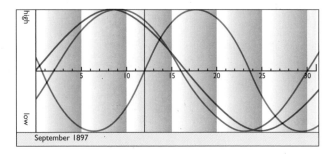

Case study: **Marie Curie on daughter Irene's birthday,** *12 September 1897*

Marie Curie was born on 7 November 1867. Her compatibility with husband Pierre was: Physical 39 per cent, Emotional 29, and Intellectual 76.

Irene was born on 12 September 1897. Her compatibility with mother Marie *(left)* was: Phy 100 per cent (competitive), Emo 29, Int 27. With her husband Frederic: Phy 91 per cent, Emo 64, Int 70. Eve was born on 6 December 1904. Her compatibility with Marie was: Phy 22 per cent , Emo 79, Int 88. With Irene: Phy 74 per cent, Emo 29, Int 88.

Pierre was born on 15 May 1859. His compatibility with Irene was: Phy 39, Emo 100, Int 52. With Eve: Phy 13 per cent, Emo 29, Int 39.

In working partnerships

Group working partnerships

Relationships at work are crucial to the well-being of the individuals and to the success of the company. Most of the research and practical applications in this area have originated in Japan. There, many firms use biorhythms to balance work relationships at all levels. As an example, personnel officers are trained to notice if one individual does not fit into their working group. This often occurs because the worker is not biorhythmically compatible with their immediate work mates. When the problem is resolved, perhaps the worker is transferred to a more suitable group, production improves.

Interestingly, in sales, the Emotional cycle seems to make an impact. Surveys of Japanese salespeople have shown that on high days in the Emotional cycle they make their sales quotas, even better them, with little effort. On low days in the Emotional cycle, these same people found they needed to use much more effort to come up to their targets. On Emotional caution days the sales force is expected to follow the rule book. The Japanese place far more importance on Emotional caution days than is done in Western countries.

Industrial and personnel managers are told not to reprimand employees on the caution days in their own Emotional cycles, as they will be 'overly emotional and not really convincing' (Professor K. Tatai, *Biorhythms for Living*). I just wonder what happens if the employee is having a 'non-receptive biorhythm day' when corrected – presumably that is taught as part of the training.

In Britain, London Underground in 1992 considered instigating a training programme, which seemed to me to be similar to the autogenic training system. Station staff would have been warned in advance of days on which they were more likely to be rude to the public. A partnership of staff and passengers was mooted.

If staff are more aware of the public, and the public respond well in return, a partnership is certainly a good idea, but if there are too few staff, even the best training efforts are wasted.

The above scheme was shelved through lack of resources, as was a scheme considered by the then British Railways Board in the early 1980s.

Individual working partnerships

In Britain, at a meeting of the CIBA Foundation in London in late 1992, the working relationships of six famous working partnerships, whose ideas impacted on a large number of people, were discussed in detail. One of these pairs was Sigmund Freud and Wilhelm Fliess (*see pages 101–102*). In each partnership it was observed that one individual was the extrovert (the front person) and that the more introvert of the two was the intellectually superior. It was felt that in each of the six examples, neither half of the partnership would have been as successful as they were if the two had not met and collaborated. Although Marie and Pierre Curie (*opposite*) were not discussed at this meeting, the same principles would apply to their family relationships.

Rudolf Nureyev and Margot Fonteyn performing in *Paradise Lost*.

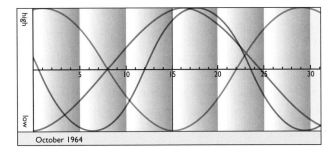

October 1964

Case study: **Rudolf Nureyev,** *15 October 1964*

Nureyev and Fonteyn

Russian ballet soloist Rudolf Nureyev was born on 17 March 1938. English prima ballerina Margot Fonteyn was born on 18 May 1919. Nureyev and Fonteyn had a very successful and long-lasting creative partnership. On 15 October 1964 they performed in *Swan Lake* at the Vienna Staatsoper, Austria, and received eighty-nine standing ovations, the greatest recorded number. Nureyev's biorhythms were HLH, and Fonteyn's were HHL.

Their biorhythm compatibility was: Physical 91 per cent, Emotional 29 per cent, and Intellectual 15 per cent. While they would usually be Physically high or low simultaneously, it would have been quite unusual for them to have four high biorhythms between them, as they had on the day of the record standing ovation, when their Viennese audience was enraptured.

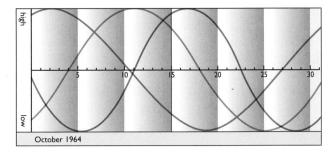

October 1964

Case study: **Dame Margot Fonteyn,** *15 October 1964*

Summary

In any creative endeavour, compatibility between partners is essential for success. In ballet, for example, the Physical cycles should be reasonably in tune, to maintain balance, and physical coordination.

The Rolling Stones in concert in London, 1995.

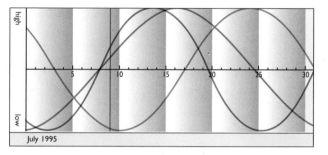

Case study: **Mick Jagger,** *9 July 1995*

Jagger and Richards

Mick Jagger was born on 26 July 1943, and Rolling Stone guitarist Keith Richards on 18 December 1943. The British phase of the Voodoo Lounge tour began in Sheffield on 9 July 1995. This two-year world tour is said to have eclipsed in earnings all previous tours by stars like Madonna, Michael Jackson and Pink Floyd.

Jagger and Richards have been working together for over thirty years. Their biorhythm compatibility is: Physical 39 per cent, Emotional 64, Intellectual 21. They have rowed many times, but their creative Emotional cycle is high. The Intellectual is quite low, so one is intuitive while the other is more practical. Their relationship has been described by some people who know them as the most important of Jagger's life. They both have homes in Richmond, Surrey.

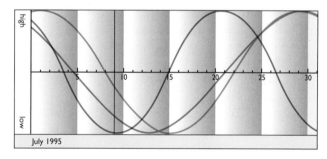

Case study: **Keith Richards,** *9 July 1995*

Summary

Biorhythm compatibility depends on a combination of biorhythms, circumstances, temperament and vested interests. If the partnership is mainly business-based, the compatibility will be mostly Intellectual.

The Apollo 13 Space Mission

Record-breaking mission

The record-breaking Apollo 13 mission to the moon left Cape Kennedy (now Cape Canaveral), Florida, on 11 April 1970, returning on 17 April. This mission still holds the record for the highest altitude achieved by man. At 1.21 am BST on 15 April 1970, they were an incredible 254 kilometres (158 miles) above the lunar surface and 400,187 kilometres (248,655 miles) above the Earth's surface.

Near disaster

The three Apollo 13 astronauts, Captain Lovell, Haise and Swigert were not really very compatible biorhythmically speaking (*see table opposite*). This mission to the moon was ill-fated, and came close to disaster. Although they broke the altitude record, they did not reach the moon. The oxygen tank exploded on 13 April. This event necessitated close teamwork during the harrowing three-and-a-half day long journey back to Earth. Fortunately, the mission team had just enough biorhythm compatibility between them to survive.

A different scenario

It could have been much worse. Swigert took the place of Thomas Matingley, born on 17 March 1936. Matingley was replaced at very short notice because he had been exposed to measles. Matingley's biorhythm compatibility with the other crew members was worse than Swigert's. Matingley's and Haise's compatibility was: Physical 74 per cent, Emotional 0 per cent and Intellectual 76 per cent. Matingley's and Lovell's: Physical 39 per cent, Emotional 86 per cent and Intellectual 39 per cent.

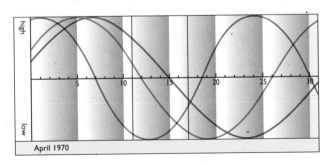

April 1970

Case study: **Captain James A. Lovell,** *mid April 1970*

Lovell, born 25 March 1928, had bad biorhythms: an Emotional caution on 12 April, Intellectual on the 15th and 16th, and Physical to come on 18th.

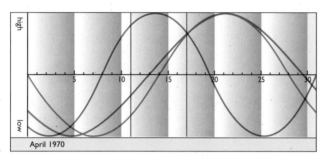

April 1970

Case study:
Fred W. Haise,
mid April 1970
Haise, born 14 November 1933, had an Intellectual caution day on 13 April and an Emotional caution day on the 14th. From 15 April he had a triple high (HHH).

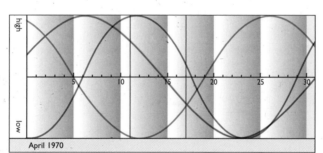

April 1970

Case study:
Jack Swigert,
mid April 1970
Swigert, born 30 August 1931, had a descending Intellectual caution day on the 14th and a Physical caution day on 17 April.

Compatibility of the crew members

	PHY	EMO	INT
Lovell and Haise:	13%	14%	15%
Lovell and Swigert:	4%	50%	94%
Haise and Swigert:	83%	64%	9%

Birth and death

From birth to death, biorhythms are part of our lives, so let us begin at the beginning of life with the birth and conception of children, to which there is a pattern.

Birth

Early in the twentieth century it was the cyclic nature of birth which led Dr Fliess and others to the discovery of biorhythms. Fliess studied the family trees of thousands of his patients across three generations before conclud-ing that natural births (by which I mean those not induced) usually occur on caution days in the Physical or Emotional biorhythms of the mother.

Emotional caution days always occur on the same weekday, so it is common for children to be born on the same weekday as their mother was. This often leads to a bunching of birthdays within a family around particular days of the week. For example, Princess Diana was born on a Saturday and her son Prince Henry was also born on a Saturday (*see Princess Diana chart below, left*).

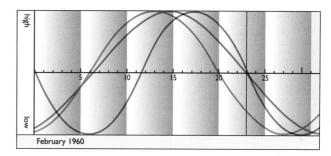

September 1984

February 1960

Case study: **Princess Diana,** *14 September 1984*

Case study: **The Empress of Japan,** *23 February 1960*

Princess Diana was born on 1 July 1961. For the birth of her second son, Prince Henry, she went into labour on a Physical caution day, 14 September 1984. He was born the next day, the 15th.

Prince William was born on 21 June 1982. His mother's biorhythms were HLH. She had experienced an Emotional caution day on 19 June and a Physical caution day on the 20th.

The Empress of Japan was born on 20 October 1934. She gave birth to the heir, Crown Prince Naruhito Hironomiya, on 23 February 1960. This was a Physical and an Intellectual caution day. Her second son, Prince Akishino, was born the day before an Intellectual caution day, and her daughter was born in a triple low.

55

Predicting the day of birth

Here are biorhythm patterns associated with birth:
• Natural birth usually occurs on caution days in the Physical and/or Emotional biorhythms of the mother.
• Birth occurs on an Emotional caution day, if the mother is particularly tense, worried or highly strung.
• Birth often occurs on an Intellectual caution day if the mother is over about thirty-four years of age.
• If there is a triple high spread over several days during the last two months of pregnancy, the mother can often expect an early, easy birth.

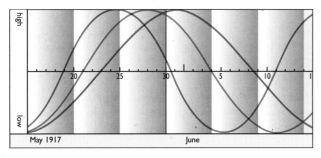

Case study: **Rose Kennedy, *30 May 1917***

Rose Kennedy, born 22 July 1890, was the mother of nine children. John Fitzgerald Kennedy was born on 30 May 1917. The future 35th President of the USA was born on a caution day in his mother's Physical cycle. This is the usual pattern for a normal birth.

'Predicting' the sex of an unborn child

Although I have called this 'predicting', it is based on knowing the biorhythm position of the mother at the time of conception. The acidity of the womb varies, and this variation affects which chromosomes (carried by the sperm) fertilize the ovum, so if the mother has a high Physical cycle and a low Emotional cycle, then the child conceived is likely to be a boy.

If the mother has a high Emotional biorhythm cycle together with a low Physical cycle, then the child is likely to be a girl.

If both the Physical and the Emotional cycles are up or down together at the time of conception, then no prediction can be made accurately.

The original study in 1904 proved this form of 'prediction' accurate in four out of five cases (about eighty per cent accuracy). This was a retrospective study carried out by Dr Fliess, but the figures have since been confirmed. It could also go some way towards explaining why there are between six and seven boys born for every five girls. However, slightly more boys than girls die in the early years of life, so it is ultimately perfectly balanced in nature.

This method of 'prediction' has a slightly higher accuracy rate than the London clinic which offers parents the probability of a child of one particular sex. Using biorhythms to predict the sex of a child, of course, involves no expense.

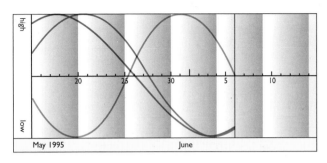

Death

Deaths, both accidental and natural, usually occur on one of the three caution days, most often the caution day in the Physical cycle. There are examples throughout the text of biorhythm sequences related to death. Professor Tatai of Japan has pointed out that when he realizes a terminally ill patient is near death, he warns the relatives of the likely date, as he feels this preparation helps them to cope with the situation.

The triple low phase is associated with natural death, usually of the elderly who die in their sleep.

Case study: **René Firino-Martell, *6 June 1995***

Firino-Martell, born 19 February 1927, was an eighth generation descendant of Jean Martell, a Jersey wine merchant who went to France and founded the company in 1715. Under Martell it became the second largest cognac house, was taken over by a multinational, and extended to 140 countries. Just before the company's 280th anniversary celebrations began, he sadly died. It was a Physical caution day with two lows (CLL).

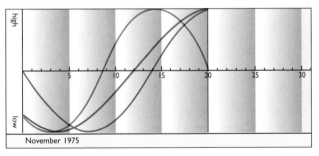

Case study: **General Franco, *20 November 1975***

General Franco of Spain, born 4 December 1892, had been in power for thirty-nine years at the time of his death. Every life-prolonging device had been used for weeks before his death. He eventually died on a Physical caution day (CHH), just after leaving a triple high period.

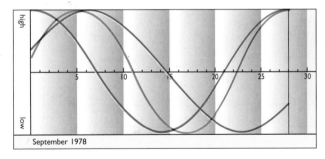

Case study: **John Paul I, *28 September 1978***

John Paul I, born 17 October 1912, died suddenly of a heart attack only thirty-three days after his election to the Papacy. It is surprising that he died on a HHL day. In 1993 a Cardinal revealed for the first time that he might not have died if two secretaries present had intervened.

Creativity

Imagination and inventiveness

Your creativity, in all its forms, is very strongly linked to the Emotional cycle. Many of the greatest songs have been composed, pictures painted, books written, inventions made, dances choreographed and every other kind of creative achievement expressed when the individual was experiencing at least a high Emotional cycle.

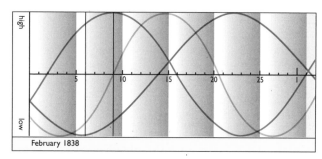

February 1838

Case study: **Charles Dickens, 6–9 February 1838**

Charles Dickens was born on 7 February 1812. By 1838 *The Pickwick Papers* and *Oliver Twist* had been published. On 7 February 1838, his twenty-sixth birthday, he announced in high spirits that he had begun writing *Nicholas Nickelby*. He started writing the night before, on the 6th. On 7 February his biorhythms were LHL, the high Emotional cycle meaning creativity, and the low Intellectual cycle indicating high intuition. Two days later, the 9th (CHL), he finished the first chapter.

Vincent Van Gogh

Van Gogh's life was one of rejection, frustration, illness – and astonishing creativity. His biorhythm chart (*opposite*) is for a year, from birthday to birthday. It was a year of great creativity and drama. Living in Arles, France, he completed about 200 paintings, 100 drawings and hundreds of letters.

In October 1888, Gauguin arrived to stay with him. However, they quarrelled and then Van Gogh threatened him. Gauguin left, Vincent cut off his ear lobe and was hospitalized the next day. He died the following year.

Van Gogh cut off his ear on a Physical caution day, which followed an Intellectual caution. This indicated a physical basis. He might have been suffering from Ménière's Disease, a condition of the inner ear, which could also have influenced his paintings.

This great artist, who 'painted with a brush of fire', linked his creative periods to the emotions: 'Is it not emotion, the sincerity of one's feeling for nature, that draws us, and if the emotions are sometimes so strong that one works without knowing one works, ... then one must remember that it has not always been so, and that in time to come there will again be hard days, empty of inspiration.' (From *Complete Letters of Vincent Van Gogh*, Vol. 2, Letter 504, © Thames & Hudson, London, 1958.)

Case study: **Vincent Van Gogh, events and a selection of his works,** *30 March 1888 to 30 March 1889*

March 1888
Completed ten paintings in the
last three weeks (HHH for much
of this period)

April 1888
*Drawbridge with Carriage
Farmers Working in Field
Basket with Potatoes*

May 1888
Rented the Yellow House, Arles;
began fixing it up
Basket with Lemons

June 1888
Went to Saintes Maries-de-la-Mer,
'travelling without weariness'
across the Carmargue.
Very productive period (HHL)
Started painting portraits

BIRTHDAY 1889
Tried to commit suicide twice
(LLL)
La Berceuse (finished)
March 1889

Deliberately antagonizing locals
(HHH)
7 Feb: hospitalized again
February 1889

*Self Portrait with Bandaged Ear
(opposite)
Dormitory in Hospital
Vase with Sunflowers*
8 Jan: began painting again
7 Jan: left hospital
January 1889

24 Dec: hospitalized
23 Dec: cut off ear lobe
23 Dec (CHC): threatened
Gauguin with his razor
14 Dec (HLH): quarrelled with
Gauguin
*Memory of the Garden at Etten
Portrait of Armand Roulin
Vincent's Chair*
December 1888

July 1888 (working hard)
*Joseph Roulin
Mousmé*
Very lonely (LLL): started
religious paintings

August 1888
*Fourteen Sunflowers in a Vase
The Old Peasant Patience Escalier
Coal Barges
Quay with Men Unloading Barges*
After 15 Aug:
Painted head of postman
Fishing Boats at Sea
'Disturbed and restless' (CCC)

September 1888
1–8 Sept (LHH):
Vincent's House (to pay rent)
*The Young Girl, The Harvest,
The Seascape*
Three paintings in a week:
*The Garden, The Night Café,
Self Portrait*
18 Sept: moved into the Yellow
House (HLL)
Café Terrace at Night

November 1888
Five portraits of postman's
family finished

October 1888
*Vincent's Bedroom
Self Portrait*
29 Oct (HHL): Gauguin arrived

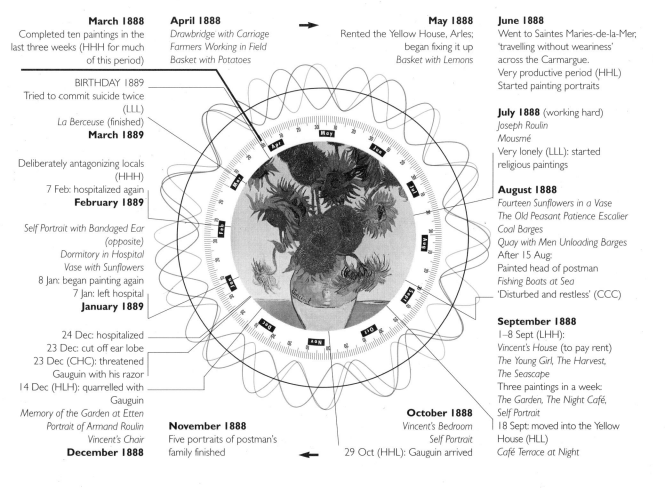

Decision making

Good decisions

Good decisions are often made when the biorhythm sequence is either two highs and a low, or all three high. The balance provided by a low cycle calms down the exuberance of two highs. There will be plenty of motivation. Do remember that the effects of biorhythms are tempered by your personality, knowledge, outlook and experiences.

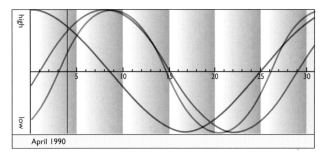

April 1990

Case study: **King Baudouin,** *4 April 1990*

King Baudouin of Belgium was born on 7 September 1930. A staunch Roman Catholic, he had wanted to become a Trappist monk. When the Belgian parliament passed an abortion law, he said he would resign rather than sign it. To avoid this, the parliament declared him 'unable to govern' for one day, 4 April 1990. The king's biorhythms were a triple high (HHH) and he made what he genuinely believed to be the right decision for him.

Bad decisions

Less wise decisions are likely to be made when the cycles are very low, or on a caution day. The position of the Emotional and Intellectual cycles is particularly important. Triple lows should always be avoided for decision making as they bring slowness of thought, and triple highs might lead to over-confidence. Decisions made on the first caution day leaving a triple high are suspect.

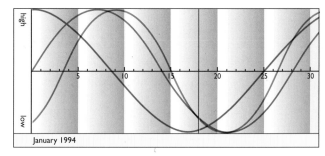

January 1994

Case study: **Michael Mates,** *18 January 1994*

British Member of Parliament, Michael Mates, born 9 June 1934, had been a Minister for Northern Ireland. He caused a major security alert at the Houses of Parliament, Westminster, when he parked a friend's car on double yellow lines, lights flashing, and left it for three hours. His explanation was that he had become involved in talks, and had forgotten about it.
This is a good example of the mental lethargy associated with a triple low phase (LLL).

Dieting

Sex drive

Plan your diet. Do not do it on impulse. Impulse decisions are related to caution days in the Intellectual cycle.
• The best time to begin a diet is when you are in a Physical high with the other cycles rising. The flow of the hormone melatonin, which regulates the body's efficiency at burning up calories, is related to certain aspects of the Physical cycle.
• Never begin a diet on an Emotional caution day.
• Always plan some non-food treats to look forward to.

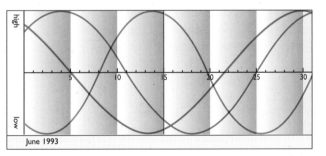

June 1993

Case study: **Oprah Winfrey,** *15 June 1993*

US television presenter Oprah Winfrey was born on 29 January 1954. In a seemingly constant battle with her weight and dieting, on 15 June 1993, she ran away to be alone because she felt she was too fat. Her biorhythms were HLL. Although the combined low Emotional and Intellectual cycles made her feel miserable and dejected, the high Physical biorhythm gave her the confidence to begin to diet again.

Popular conception associates sex drive with a high Physical cycle, when people feel sexier and more confident in themselves, and so are more likely to want sex and to have sex. The high Physical gives both the motivation and the energy, but is this the only influence?

There has been little research on biorhythms and sex, except for the compatibility aspect (*see pages 41–47*). Marriages or relationships that have a very high Physical biorhythm compatibility tend to be dramatic and short-lived. However, it is a powerful bond, and couples who experience this are often drawn to each other again and again, rather like an obsession.

Whether the Physical biorhythm is the only influence on the quality as well as the quantity of sexual activity, I leave to readers to decide for themselves.

Education, exams, interviews

Days of exams and interviews are not usually of our choosing. Bear the following points in mind, especially if there is a choice of dates, as with a driving test.

Advice for children

Since the mid 1970s much of the Japanese education system has become biorhythm-orientated. Here is some advice provided by educator Yoshiyuki Okimura for parents of children who are preparing to do a test or exam.

- For at least four days before any exam, regardless of the child's biorhythms, give them nourishing foods that are high in vitamin C (combats stress) and in the vitamin B complex (builds up the nervous system). Check that the child is not suffering from diarrhoea brought on by nervous tension. I would also consider giving the child Bach Rescue Remedy (*see page 109*).

- To ease worry, familiarize the child with the examination room by taking them to the building several times.

- Children should not be taught complicated new subjects during a low phase in the Emotional cycle. Allow more play during these periods, because play is creative.

- During the low Emotional phases, place more emphasis on repetitive skills, like learning languages, vocabularies and multiplication tables.

- During a high Emotional cycle, children become bored and restless more easily.

Relevant points to note in the cycles

The diagram below highlights some aspects of research linking children and learning. The effect of biorhythms on learning may vary according to the age, temperament and motivation of the child. Compatibility between teacher and child is also very important.

- On caution days in the Emotional biorhythm, younger children become niggling and irritable, and go to sleep earlier than normal.

- Under the age of ten, the learning of complicated new facts should be restricted to the high Emotional biorhythm phases.

Adults: driving test

• Try to take your test when you have two high bio-rhythms, the most important being a high Physical cycle. The learner is 'on show' to the examiner and needs to appear confident, whatever the reality. In Britain, a driving school in Hythe, Cheshire has used biorhythms for years to select test dates to increase the pass rate. First time passes rose considerably.

Case study: Sue Brown, failed test, *14 January 1994*

Secretary Sue Brown was born on 5 November 1957. She took her second driving test on 14 January 1994. Her biorhythms were LHL. The low Physical biorhythm meant a lack of confidence, particularly after her previous failure, the low Intellectual cycle dulled her mental reactions, and the high Emotional cycle meant that she was on edge and did some very creative driving.

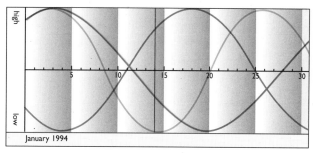

January 1994

Case study: Sue Brown, passed, *19 November 1994*

Sue Brown took her third test on 19 November 1994. By this time she had learned about biorhythms and chose a more compatible driving instructor and her own test date. She passed. Her biorhythms were HHL. The high Physical gave her confidence, and compensated for the high Emotional. She allowed for the low Intellectual by having an early night before the test.

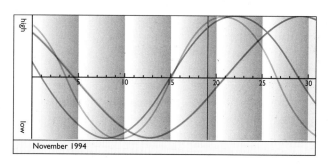

November 1994

Adults: helpful advice for exams and interviews

- Do not panic. Try to relax. Breathe deeply and calmly at all times of potential stress.
- Remember that, all other things being equal, the people who do well in exams are those who consistently keep a cool head.
- Do everything you can to tilt the balance of events in your favour. Try to get an early night.
- If you have worked well in the run up to an exam, you are ahead.
- Allow extra time for everything. This way, you will not have to worry if something unexpected happens.
- Check the route to your examination or interview. If necessary, do a trial run.
- The night before, double-check your pens, pencils, other instruments and calculator batteries. This sounds simple but most people do not do it. A friend of mine had to wait a year to resit his Master of Science examination: he thought he had changed his calculator batteries, but had forgotten to put the new ones in.
- Unless you are particularly unlucky, there should be something good in the biorhythm chart for you to focus on. Look for this and emphasize your likely strengths.
- If there really are not any biorhythm assets to back you up, or if you feel that you need a 'natural' boost, I suggest the use of Bach Rescue Remedy or another Bach combination (*see Information and Addresses, page 109*).

Research:

USA: One study of four students covering a total of fifteen subjects over a fourteen-month period. This study found that grades attained were far better when students were in the positive phases of the cycles, with the Intellectual cycle having special significance.

West Germany: A retrospective study showed that eighty-three per cent of failures occurred when the individual had a low Intellectual biorhythm, and that grades were lower when two or three cycles were low together.

Points in the cycles to note:

Research has shown that we are more likely to succeed in exams, tests or interviews when our biorhythms are in certain patterns. Even if we cannot choose the day, by referring to our chart we can plan ahead to compensate for a less-than-good day.

• For those with a more determined attitude to life, a high Intellectual cycle would be most useful, especially if you believe in mind over matter. If you believe yourself to be ambitious, a high Intellectual biorhythm is preferable to a high Emotional one.

• The Intellectual cycle: the more intelligent the individual, the more noticeable the difference generally is between the high and the low phases of this cycle, with particular emphasis on caution-day errors.

• Those with a nervous or highly strung disposition should try to sit an exam during a high Physical biorhythm (helps regulate confidence) and a low Emotional biorhythm (helps prevent over-reacting).

• The Emotional cycle: during a low phase, an introverted person studying for long periods will become gloomy, moody and insecure. This could lay the foundation for future bouts of depression.

Health and illness

Since the turn of the twentieth century, it has been noted that health and certain illnesses can be correlated with either the Physical or the Emotional biorhythms.

Resistance to and recovery from illness

Children

Dr Fliess observed that children exposed to measles on the same day had an incubation period of up to six days, becoming ill on the next Physical caution day; siblings could succumb several days apart. Vulnerable children, or those exposed to disease, are more likely to contract an illness on their Physical caution day.

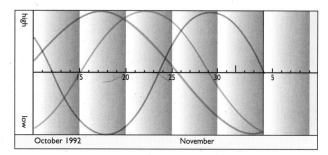

Case study: **Master John Lonsdale, *4 November 1992***

The death of Princess Diana's godson, John, born 14 November 1991, was termed as a 'cot death'. It was a Physical caution day with the other cycles at their lowest. Is there a link between biorhythms and cot deaths?

Adults

Dr Fliess noted that the onset of colds and flu in adults followed the same pattern. In the winter, take extra vitamins and get more rest before a Physical caution day.

ME (*Myalgic encephalomyelitis*) is now being acknowledged. It is characterized by severe muscle fatigue after any exertion. Although the cause is unknown, it may be brought on by a persistent viral infection. The onset may coincide with Physical and Emotional caution days.

Immunization

Take positive action to ensure that your immunization is trouble-free and less stressful.

Advice
• Choose a high phase in the Physical cycle.
• If possible, choose another high cycle too.
• A high Intellectual cycle (reasoning power) is beneficial, if you are particularly worried by injections.
• It is important to avoid Physical caution days: indeed all caution days should be avoided.

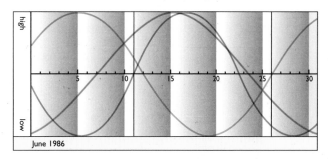

Dentistry

Anything that makes having dental work a happier experience is to be welcomed.

Advice

- Avoid major dental work on any caution day.
- Choose a day when as many biorhythm cycles as possible are high. If this is not possible, try to choose a high in the Physical cycle.
- Sudden toothache is usually correlated to caution days in the Emotional (Sensitivity) cycle.

Research

Japan: Dental surgeon Mr Hiroshi Tani took a sample of 700 patients from the time before he began to use biorhythms; there were bad effects or complications in 80 per cent of extractions 'carried out on the patients' caution days'. Of the remaining 20 per cent (those not having a caution day), 99 per cent experienced no bad effects during dental treatment. Of patients who came for the treatment of abscesses, 80 per cent were experiencing caution days at the time, the majority being caution days in the Physical cycle, when pain is most acute.
Europe: Biorhythms have been used in dentistry in Europe since before the Second World War (Tatai).

Case study: **Mrs Covington, 11, 26 June 1986**

Mrs Covington was born on 17 July 1924. On 11 June 1986 (CHH) a brain haemorrhage led to a coma.

After fifteen days, on the 26th (LCL), she regained consciousness and made a complete recovery.

Coma

Coma sufferers tend to recover consciousness on caution days in the Emotional cycle (*see charts above and below*).

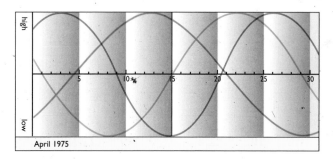

Case study: **Karen Ann Quinlan, 15 April 1975**

Karen was born on 16 March 1954. A combination of tranquillizers and alcohol on 15 April 1975 (LCH) left her in a ten-year coma. [Support machines were switched off in March 1976. On 12 June 1985 (HCL) she died.]

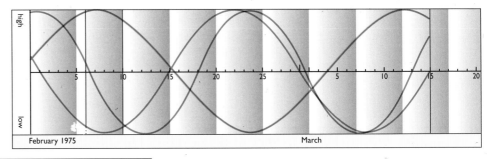

February 1975   March

Routine surgery

General advice

• Avoid any caution day, especially a caution day in the Physical cycle.
• Then pick as many high cycles as feasible, paying particular attention to the Physical cycle.

Research

Switzerland: By avoiding operating on all caution days, Dr Fritz Wehrli claimed a record of more than 10,000 routine operations performed without post-operative complications. This research occurred at his clinic in Locarno between 1945 and the mid-1970s. This record is remarkable when compared with the World Health Organization (WHO) statistic of one patient in five suffering from post-operative complications in the USA and some European countries in the 1980s. The comparison is not absolute because the WHO figures cover all medical operations, not just routine ones, but is still very favourable to biorhythms.

Japan: Professor Tatai has noted that research has shown that bleeding is far more profuse on a caution day in the Physical biorhythm.

Case study: **Aristotle Onassis, _6, 10 February 1975_**

Onassis, born 20 January 1906, hated doctors. He had been under pressure. His son had died in a plane crash. A divorce from Jackie was rumoured. For months he had known that he needed a gallbladder operation. He finally agreed to this on 6 February 1975 (CLH). Physical caution days always make pain seem worse. The operation was on 10 February (LLH). He died on 15 March 1975 (HCH), an Emotional caution day.

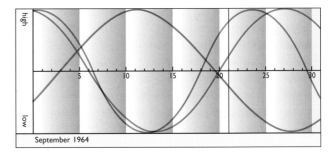

September 1964

Case study: **Bikila Abebe, _21 September 1964_**

Athlete Bikila Abebe of Ethiopia was born on 7 August 1932. He had an appendix operation on 21 September (HHL) when his Physical and Emotional biorhythms were rising. A month after the operation he won a Gold medal in the Tokyo Olympics.

Heart attacks, strokes, high blood pressure

There seem to be specific biorhythm patterns associated with heart attacks and strokes. Being aware of these patterns could save the life of someone vulnerable.

Heart attacks

People who have the predisposition to heart attacks or strokes are most vulnerable on Physical caution days or on double caution days.

Points to note in the biorhythms:

- Vulnerable people are most at risk on CHH and CLL days. Such people are those who have probably persistently abused their bodies over the years, or have taken too many different medicines over a short period. The latter example nearly always happens on a CHH day.
- In some cases, a minor heart attack can be aggravated by the stresses created by the worrying patient.
- In the case above, or when the first heart attack has produced complications or left permanent damage, the patient is most susceptible to a second, often more serious heart attack. This usually happens on the next caution day in the Physical cycle. In other words, there will be a gap of eleven or twelve days between the two incidents (*see Clark Gable chart, right*).

Sadly, the number of heart attacks is increasing, and contrary to popular belief women are now just as susceptible to heart attacks as men. One way of reducing the risk of heart disease is to try not to smoke.

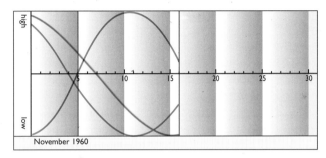

November 1960

Case study: **Clark Gable, 5, 16 November 1960**

In his book *Is this Your Day?*, American biorhythm expert George Thommen began by recalling the public warning he had once given the film star Clark Gable regarding his health.

At the time of the warning, Gable, born 1 February 1901, was in hospital. He had had a heart attack on a Physical caution day (CLH) while filming *The Misfits*, co-starring Marilyn Monroe.

George Thommen was being interviewed on *The Long John Nebel Show*, broadcast by a radio station in New York City. On 11 November 1960 George Thommen told listeners that Clark Gable could be in mortal danger from a second heart attack on 16 November 1960, the next Physical caution day (CLL) following the his heart attack. That indeed happened. It was later discovered that emergency resuscitation equipment which might have saved Clark Gable's life had been removed from his hospital room when staff believed that he seemed to be making good progress.

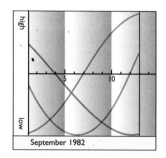 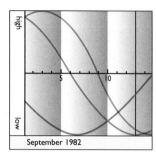

September 1982   September 1982

Strokes

A stroke is a temporary suspension of blood to a part or parts of the brain, causing damage. Strokes can vary in intensity. In about half the cases a complete recovery can be made.

Strokes tend to occur on either a double caution day in the Physical and Emotional cycles (most usual pattern) or on a Physical caution day combined with a low Emotional biorhythm.

Advice

• When it is realized that a person is susceptible to heart attacks or strokes, the dates on which they might occur can be calculated. I have used this technique effectively while chronicling the recurrence of mini-strokes in an elderly relative, who thankfully recovered completely after each episode.
• The flow of blood to the brain can be restricted by surprisingly simple things, such as an elderly man tying his neck tie too tightly, or a lady wearing a tight necklace or scarf. This can easily happen when a person's reactions might be dulled through tension or heightened by excitability.
• The elderly are particularly vulnerable on important and stressful days like birthdays, weddings or other family gatherings, especially when alcohol is available.
• Both strokes and heart attacks usually occur on caution days in the Physical biorhythm.

Case study: **Princess Grace and Princess Stephanie of Monaco,** *13 September 1982*

Princess Grace was born on 12 November 1929. She was driving with her younger daughter, Princess Stephanie *(below)*, between Nice and Monaco when she had a stroke at the wheel, the car crashed, and she died (HHL). The stroke was not initially reported or mentioned. It occurred one day after a Physical caution day *(above, left)*. This could be accounted for by the fact that she died more than five time zones away from the place where she was born. However, as was rumoured at the time, Princess Stephanie, born February 1965, may have been driving (LLL). She was one year under-age and did not have a driving licence. Compare her chart *(above, right)* with that of Michael Mates *(see page 60)*.

'Stupidity', absent-mindedness

I am using the word 'stupidity' here as a very general term covering a number of 'crazy' situations. 'Stupidity' can be Physical, Emotional or Intellectual, and can be associated with any caution day or a triple low, when dull-wittedness may be attributed to tiredness.

Physical 'stupidity'

We may appear to be 'stupid' when our reactions are slow. Since reaction times are governed by the autonomic nervous system, incidents of Physical 'stupidity' are associated with caution days in the Physical cycle.

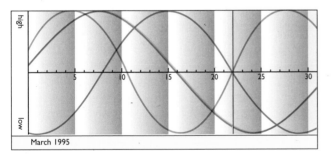

March 1995

Case study: **Christopher Heath,** *22 March 1995*

Racing enthusiast Christopher Heath was born on 26 September 1946. On 22 March 1995 (CCL) he unexpectedly failed to arrive to see the Cheltenham Gold Cup race. The phone rang while he was in the bath; he got up to answer it, fell and broke several ribs.

Emotional 'stupidity'

Emotional 'stupidity' occurs when there is an emotional or irrational outburst. If someone over-reacts to a very small incident, we tell them 'not to be so stupid'. Emotional 'stupidity' is associated with caution days in the Emotional biorhythm, often combined with a second caution day or perhaps two low cycles.

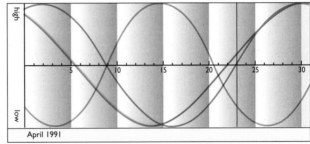

April 1991

Case study: **Gerald Ratner,** *23 April 1991*

Gerald Ratner was born on 1 November 1949. The entrepreneur was chairman of a jewellery company named after him. While addressing a lunch at a convention of the Institute of Directors, he memorably said that Ratner's jewellery was 'absolute crap' and that Marks and Spencer's prawn sandwiches were better value. His injudicious remarks were widely and repeatedly quoted in the press. Sales in Ratner shops plummeted, and he was forced to resign as chairman (see page 72).

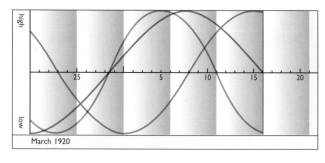

March 1920

Case study: **Edith Holden,** *16 March 1920*

Edith Holden was born on 26 September 1871. She was an illustrator and naturalist. Many years after her death *The Country Diary of an Edwardian Lady* became famous. While walking beside the River Thames at Kew, near London, she saw an overhanging branch of flowering chestnut, which she wanted to paint. She went to pick it, fell in the river and drowned. It was an Intellectual caution day with a low Physical and high Emotional (excitability) cycle.

To illustrate Emotional 'stupidity', first refer to the characteristics of an LCH day (*see page 34*). Then look closely at the Gerald Ratner chart (*see page 71*). This is a particularly interesting chart.

The mental adaptability needed to realize the effect of what he was actually saying was not there. The Intellectual cycle had only just begun to rise at this point in his chart. If he had given his speech two days later, it would have made all the difference.

Note that by 23 April 1991 there had been consecutive caution days from 20 to 23 April with the effect of four caution days in a three-day period. Here the characteristics of LCH days are heightened by the build-up of biorhythm effects from the previous days. This could only exacerbate any situation.

Gerald Ratner's experience is a dramatic example of the effects of a sequence of caution days, when life can be suddenly and inexorably altered. He is shown here in one of his retail shops before his resignation.

Intellectual 'stupidity'

The Intellectual biorhythm was discovered by Dr Alfred Teltscher (*see page 103*), who had observed the occasional slow-witted behaviour of even the brightest of his students. This led him to the conclusion that intellectual abilities must be cyclic.

In incidents of Intellectual 'stupidity' the brain is dulled (*see chart above*), leading to slow-thinking or absent-mindedness. We may forget or lose things, or say something which, even as we speak, the brain is telling us is the wrong thing to say.

Absent-mindedness occurs on Intellectual caution days, especially if other cycles are low, or caution days.

Note: Intellectual 'stupidity' includes shop-lifting and suicide (*see pages 73–4*).

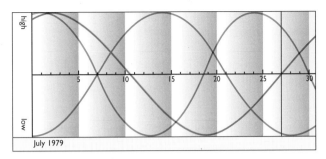

July 1979

Shop-lifting, deliberate

Shop-lifting by a professional thief is usually associated with a high phase in the Physical cycle. The thief who weighs up the possibility of success and then decides to act relies on a high personal confidence factor.

Shop-lifting, accidental

This occurs through absent-mindedness, which is associated with a caution day in the Intellectual cycle. Intellectual 'stupidity', as expressed in shop-lifting, is very easy to understand in oneself or others. We have all at one time or another done something which, at the time, we had no logical reason to do. We might say ourselves that we were 'absolutely crazy' when we did it.

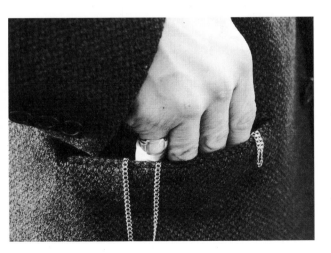

Case study: **James Dunn, *27 July 1979***

British MP James Dunn was born on 30 January 1926. On 27 July 1979 (HLC), the Cabinet Minister left the Houses of Parliament having been up all night debating in the House. He went into a store in Westminster and walked out with a ballpoint pen. The shop prosecuted him for shop-lifting even though the monetary value was low. This is an example of accidental shop-lifting.

Intuition

Intuition is a suspension of one's rational mind. In many respects it is a positive form of absent-mindedness.

Flashes of intuition are related to caution days in the Intellectual cycle, and, when these occur on double caution days with the Emotional cycle, they can instigate brilliant and accurate flashes of insight.

Biorhythms depend on the circumstances and personality of the individual. This intuitive response is correlated to the same biorhythm patterns which, in unstable individuals, result in suicide.

There are many examples of inspired wins, for example at the races, associated with double caution days in the Emotional and Intellectual cycles, usually when the Physical cycle is also high.

For less pleasant associations see the next page.

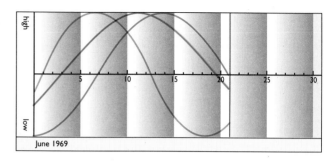

June 1969

Suicide

Suicide is a conscious and violent act involving the Intellectual and/or Physical biorhythms. As biorhythms can provide a positive preventative measure, which costs nothing, I have given this a lot of thought.

Broadly speaking, suicides can be divided into two groups: suicides resulting from a shock to, or a lack of, confidence (Physical caution days), and suicides resulting from long-term unhappiness or mental instability (Intellectual/Emotional double caution days, LCC or HCC). The latter are planned, and can be anticipated.

Circumstances: suicide or accident?

These points should lead to accurate assessments of the circumstances leading to death:

Suicide, drug- or alcohol-related: on an Emotional caution day, with an Intellectual caution day either immediately before or after this, would almost certainly be a suicide attempt. (*See Garland chart, above.*)

Suicide, not drug-related: on a Physical caution day. This would be associated with people with no self-esteem. Death is by violent means such as hanging.

Death by accidental overdose: on an Emotional caution day, with a high Physical, could be an accidental overdose due to brashness/emotional weakness.

Accidental death due to exuberance: a rarer occurrence – at least two biorhythm cycles are high, with no caution days. This is more likely to be accidental.

Case study: **Judy Garland, *21 June 1969***

Judy Garland was born 10 June 1922. The mother of Liza Minnelli had herself been a major star from childhood. In later life, the well-loved singer became a sad but still compelling figure. On 21 June 1969 she overdosed and died. It was an Emotional caution day (LCL), immediately preceded by an Intellectual caution day.

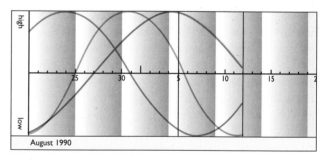

August 1990

Case study: **'Simon', *5, 12 August 1990***

'Simon', was born on 5 September 1972. His story was featured on BBC Radio 4. This timid teenager, with no malice in him, took to petty crime. He was sent to an adult prison on remand, where, after a few days, he took his life. He was almost 18 years old. His suicide attempt (hanging) was on 5 August (CLH). On 12 August (LLC) he died without regaining consciousness.

Addiction

On Physical caution days we tend to lack confidence. Seeking the comfort and support of alcohol or drugs may, at first, appear helpful. The cycle of addiction begins when a person gradually pushes up their intake of any habit-forming substance. The body quickly accepts this as its normal ration and sends the brain messages that more is required.

Alcohol addiction

The body metabolizes alcohol in a similar way to the way it uses food. Basically alcohol is a carbohydrate and is absorbed in the stomach. The body uses food most effectively when the Physical cycle is high. When the Physical cycle is low, or on a caution day, the same amount of alcohol is slower to take effect, so a delayed reaction builds up without the drinker being aware of it. So they drink still more to try to achieve the same effect.

Substance addiction (both prescription medicine and unlawful drugs)

The same general principle applies to tablets taken by mouth. On Physical caution days reactions are slow or dulled, so the effects of a substance are delayed, the individual becomes impatient, takes a booster, but they have already had enough. The substance has not absorbed efficiently, but it is still there because it has been consumed. An impatient or impetuous person can easily overdose.

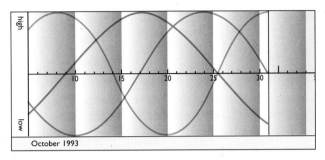

October 1993

Case study: **River Phoenix, *31 October 1993***

Promising young actor River Phoenix was born on 23 August 1970. From the age of ten he had been an actor, starring in: *Mosquito Coast*; *Running on Empty,* for which he was nominated for an Academy Award as best supporting actor in 1988; and *My Own Private Idaho* in 1991. On 31 October 1993, after leaving the Viper Room club in Los Angeles, he collapsed on the sidewalk, and died from a drugs overdose. His biorhythms were HCL.

Research

UK: It has been noted that the day before the 29th birthday has a particular significance for suicide attempts. There is a much higher number of suicide attempts on this day (CHL) than on any other day in a person's life. The reason for this pattern is not yet understood.

75

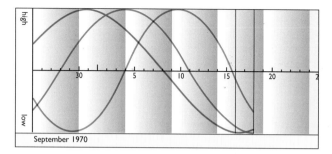

September 1970

Case study: Jimi Hendrix, *16, 18 September 1970*

Rock guitarist Jimi Hendrix was born 27 November 1942. At the inquest into his death, evidence was given that he had taken nine strong sleeping tablets throughout the night of 16 September; these had not sent him to sleep. The 15 Sept was a Physical caution day (CLL) with a double-day effect.

After he collapsed, he was taken from the Isle of Wight Pop Festival, where he had been playing, to the London hospital in which he died on 18 September (LLL). The verdict was an open one. *(See page 75 regarding delayed effect.)* Compare Jimi Hendrix's death with that of Elvis *(page 33).*

Does someone really want to change?

If you really wish to break your habit, you must want to change your situation. A half-hearted attempt will only reinforce any feelings of inadequacy.

Accidental drug overdoses are most likely to occur on Physical or Emotional caution days (over-exuberance).

Note: someone who has no intention of changing their lifestyle, or who is foolish enough to try drugs for the first time, must avoid all caution days and triple low phases. These times are even more dangerous. First-time drug users can die or be permanently injured. It was Karen Anne Quinlan's first 'mixture' *(see page 67).*

Beginning withdrawal

If this is what you really want, and you are ready to begin, plan your withdrawal so **you** are in control. Success is then more likely.

- Physical cycle: choose a rising caution day. That first day will be hard – no doubt about it – but you know that in advance. Once that day is over, you will be on the up.
- Intellectual cycle: choose a day when this cycle is high to increase your will-power. Remember, you are doing this because you want to do it.
- Emotional cycle: the best position will depend on your personality. If you have a depressed or morose side, pick a high Emotional biorhythm day. This will help buoy you up when you need the emotional support. If you have a highly strung temperament, aim for a low period in this cycle to reduce the amount of over-reaction and irritation you experience. This should help you to get through the first day.
- Caution days in the Emotional cycle: definitely avoid these days when beginning withdrawal. Beginning on this day would guarantee failure.
- Try to be in a place where you can be quiet and on your own. (No one will see you in a bad light.)
- Plan something you can really look forward to for the second day of withdrawal.

Accidents and biorhythms

Many accidents could be avoided if people noted their Physical caution days, and were much more careful.

In the home: children

On a Physical caution day, the child could pull something onto himself or drink something poisonous.

Advice to mothers

• Take particular care on **your** Intellectual caution days; it is easy to leave things within a child's reach.

• If at home with your children, be prepared for **their** Emotional caution days, when they are most likely to be irritating. You could well be at a low ebb too and feel unable to cope. Knowing there is a reason for disruptive or destructive behaviour could mean the difference between you 'snapping' or being able to take the situation in your stride. Grandparents or friends can be of enormous help with a difficult child.

Research

Japan: Children and caution days in the Physical and Emotional cycles (researcher Mr Okimura):

• Children tend to become sick or injured; or more inclined to tease or bully younger children.

• In city areas there were more incidences of petty crime and playing with fire. In country areas, children stole and got into more mischief.

Mr Okimura's conclusions: children work out more of their frustrations and resentments on Physical and Emotional caution days. He believes the Intellectual cycle starts at birth, but does not develop, and is not clinically observable, until puberty, because children have underdeveloped nervous and endocrine gland systems until they are at least ten years old. This could explain why this cycle was not observed by Fliess (*page 101*).

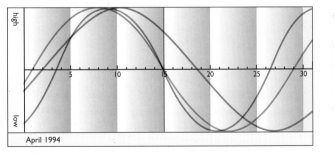

April 1994

Case study: **Angela Kent,** *15 April 1994*

Angela Kent was born on 12 December 1969. The harassed mother shut the kitchen door and trapped her toddler's fingers. Angela was late and her biorhythms were on a double caution day, descending from a triple high (CCH). This pattern made her fraught. Luckily, none of the child's fingers were broken. On a CCH day do not try to do too much. Allow yourself extra time.

In the home: adults

The main cause of accidents to adults in the home is falls, and they often have serious consequences.

If you are alone a lot, try to take note of your Physical caution days. Be very careful and observant on these days because you will not be thinking or reacting as quickly as usual.

Falls involve an overbalance which is probably one's own fault, and they correlate highly with caution days in the Physical biorhythm. Interestingly, slipping and tripping occur twice as often when the Physical cycle is low rather than high. Trips and slips seldom happen on caution days in any cycle.

Many elderly people fall out of bed on a Physical caution day. Their autonomic nervous system temporarily fails them and they misjudge the distance to the floor when they get up. A carer should take note of Physical caution days.

Other accidents in the home, garden and garage cover a wide spectrum of activities. These range from falling asleep under a sun lamp, to being electrocuted by the electric lawn-mower; from being burned by barbecue lighter fluid, to cutting off a finger with tools; or even confusing your medication or using the wrong cooking ingredient. (*See Heath chart, page 71.*)

On caution days, you need to take particular care and try to allow time for double-checking everything that you do, because you are not thinking clearly.

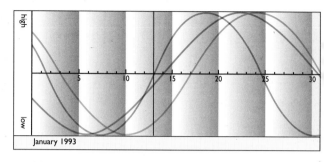

January 1993

Case study: **The Lord Runcie,** *13 January 1993*

Lord Runcie, the former Archbishop of Canterbury, was born on 2 October 1921. He was planning a lecture tour of Australia. When he was getting his suitcase down, he stood on a chair, then suddenly fell and broke his heel (CLL). The trip had to be cancelled because his foot was in plaster. Falling from a chair is a very common accident in the home.

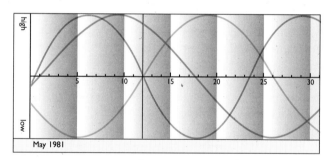

May 1981

Case study: **Stuart Hall,** *12 May 1981*

Stuart Hall was born on 25 December 1934. He was host of BBC TV's *It's a Knockout*. On this day (CCH) he fell asleep at home under his sun lamp. He was taken to hospital with general burns. This occurred on a Physical and Emotional caution day. It is a good example of the kind of accident that might happen on a Physical caution day.

Travel

Cars

There are three main categories of driving accident, and probably accidents in general.

Accidents result from:

- Over-confidence and/or slowness of reactions.
- Loss of concentration for a few moments.
- Tiredness, illness or stress.

From a biorhythm viewpoint, all of these causes correlate with: a caution day in the Physical cycle; a caution day in the Intellectual cycle; or when the biorhythms in general are exceptionally low. When we at the London Biorhythm Company analyzed the questionnaires we hold on driving (and motorcycle) accidents, it was soon obvious that the largest number of those accidents involved a caution day in the Physical cycle and were caused by young men under the age of approximately twenty-eight years.

The information suggests that young men take (and subconsciously realize that they take) unnecessary risks. These include: overtaking when the time available is too short to ensure safety; driving while under the influence of drugs or alcohol; and not being aware of pedestrians (Intellectual caution day). To combat the risk of accidents, try to make sure that your blood sugar is sufficiently high, and rest at least once every two hours.

Competing in cars or motorcycles combines both sporting biorhythms and travel biorhythms (*see Freddie Spencer chart, page 28; Lawrence of Arabia chart, page 38*).

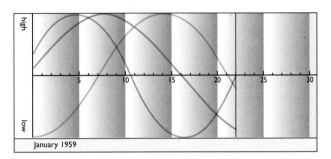

January 1959

Case study: **Mike Hawthorne, *22 January 1959***

World champion racing driver Mike Hawthorne, born 10 April 1929, had announced his retirement from motor racing only a few days before his fatal accident. On a wet road near London, his 3.4 litre Jaguar spun out of control on a Physical caution day. His biorhythm position on 22 January 1959 was CLL.

Grand Prix drivers who have died in active racing include Italian Giunti Cabantous (HHC) and New Zealander Jerry Hoyt (LLL).

Drivers steering into cyclists

Another group of motoring accidents that correlates with the Intellectual biorhythm involves motorists turning into cyclists without apparently noticing that they are there. These accidents tend to happen in bad weather, low light, or when the driver is impatient. These motoring accidents usually happen on routes which the driver knows well.

Skidding

Skidding in a vehicle comes under the same category as falls (*see page 78*). It is normally associated with a Physical caution day (lack of the ability to control the car).

Crossing the central reservation, then driving the wrong way

Accidents involving Intellectual caution days occur when, in a split second, the driver loses concentration and all sense of place. They might even cross the central reservation, and drive the wrong way down a motorway, simply because they are in a state of confusion. Actress Jayne Mansfield died in this type of accident. This can be exacerbated by alcohol.

Research

Germany: In the 1960s, for car accidents in some states in Germany, drivers' biorhythms were taken into consideration, when drink-driving, vehicle defects or injuries, or a disagreement as to the responsibility of each driver, were not involved. The balance of probability favoured of the driver whose biorhythms were not on a caution day.

UK: Studies have been undertaken to show whether there is any connection between the biorhythms of the driver and motor accidents. The Nottinghamshire County Council survey concluded there was one.

To avoid having a driving accident:

● On a caution day in the Physical cycle: pay special attention to the speed at which you are travelling, because you many not realize how fast you are going. Consider your condition to be that of a person who has taken a moderate amount of alcohol, even if you have not had a drink.

● On Emotional caution days: try not to annoy other road users.

In Britain, connections between motor accidents and single caution days in the Emotional cycle are rare, although in Japan this combination is more common. When motor accidents do occur on Emotional caution days, they are usually attributable to irritability or frustration, and nearly always follow immediately after a triple high phase.

● On an Intellectual caution day: be careful. Pay extra attention to road signs and signals. People on pedestrian crossings are a major hazard at this time.

● HHC days: minor car accidents often occur. These usually involve silly lapses of memory, like leaving the hand brake off, ramming another car from the rear or just leaving the car unlocked.

● On Physical caution days: make sure that you have enough rest and regular breaks. Keep your sugar level up by snacking. Most road accidents occur when the driver is overtired.

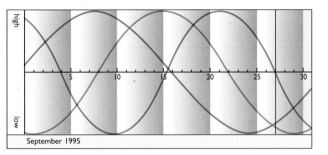

September 1995

Case study: **Michael Schumacher, *27 September 1995***

World Formula One Driving Champion, German Michael Schumacher, was born on 3 January 1969. While driving on the autobahn, he was fiddling with his radio, did not see the traffic slow down, and hit the corner of a truck. This minor accident happened on a CLL day (slow reactions) and he admitted momentary loss of concentration. Luckily no serious damage was done to either vehicle.

Planes

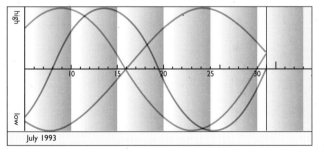

July 1993

Case study: **Ed Jones, *31 July 1993***

Family man, Ed Jones was born on 22 May 1959. On 31 July 1993 (CHH) his hang-glider hit power lines in Kent. He would have had three caution days in a row.

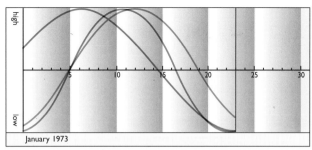

January 1973

Case study: **Alexander Onassis, *23 January 1973***

The only son of Aristotle Onassis, Alexander, was born on 30 April 1948. Exhilarated at squeezing concessions from his father on his forthcoming marriage and other things, he was in a hurry to get to London. The new private pilot was tired, having just flown the plane in to Athens. Despite this, Alexander and the pilot did the safety checks themselves and took off without having had a sufficient rest. They crashed shortly after leaving Athens and both men unfortunately died. Alexander was experiencing a triple low (LLL) biorhythm phase, while the pilot had a caution day in the Physical cycle.

Research
USA and Canada: On a Physical caution day reactions of trained pilots were six times slower compared to pilots with a Physical high (Willis).

By 1973 United Airlines were using their computers to chart the biorhythms of 28,000 ground staff and maintenance crews. Proctor and Gamble paper products at Green Bay, Wisconsin, were using biorhythms charts for their employees. Many Canadian companies were also using biorhythms to enhance performance at work.

In commerce and industry

The application of the knowledge of biorhythms can have a positive impact on commerce and industry. Many surveys have been undertaken by industrial companies in a number of countries, often sponsored by insurance companies who thus save on claims. The first such survey was carried out in Zurich, Switzerland, as far back as 1939. The Swiss are still keen on biorhythms today.

Using an understanding of biorhythms to reduce accidents (*see research opposite*) can, and is, having a beneficial effect, thus sparing human misery and saving both individuals and companies large amounts of production time and money. There is hardly a country in the industrialized world in which biorhythm studies involving industrial accidents and productivity have not been carried out. Initially, large companies avoided publicity on this subject, but they are now more open.

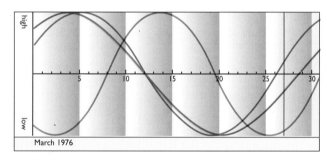

March 1990

March 1976

Case study: **Alan Bond,** *16 , 23 March 1990*

Case study: **Anita Roddick,** *27 March 1976*

Australian businessman, Alan Bond, was born on 22 April 1938. Bond Corporation Holdings was in trouble by late1989. He had bought Van Gogh's *Irises* in 1987 for a record price. He decided to sell it on 11 January 1990 (HLC), and did so at a loss on 16 March (HCH). He tried unsuccessfully to sell the Hong Kong interests on 23 March (CHL, no confidence). [On 31 August 1990 (CCC) he relinquished total company control.]

Anita Roddick, was born on 23 October 1942. She opened her first Body Shop in Brighton, England, on 27 March 1976. Earlier in the month, when she most needed it, she had had a creative double high followed by a triple high phase. Her views on women and cosmetics met the mood of the time. She and her husband now control a business empire worth millions. Their future plans include setting up a charitable trust.

Biorhythms and accident prevention research

USA: Mr R. K. Anderson of Russell K. Anderson Associates, was a consultant registered with the American Board of Industrial Hygiene. He believes that, 'Those of us who are in the field of accident prevention are constantly looking for the cause of an accident, and despite intense investigation we may find no other cause than the carelessness of the workman, who in most cases is as thoroughly confused as to why the accident happened.'

Mr Anderson ran a two-year study of all 300 accidents in four factories in four different industries. All of these accidents were covered by the Workman's Compensation Board, and they were therefore described in full detail.

Researchers were amazed to find that seventy per cent of the accidents occurred on caution days. Of those remaining, one man born in the Far East (different time zone) had had a number of accidents. His biorhythms were one day off a Physical caution. When the date was adjusted, these accidents, too, occurred on caution days. (*See Princess Grace chart, page 70.*)

Another man, on a triple high, tried to lift far more than the legally permitted limit 'because he was feeling so good' and thought he could manage safely. This resulted in permanent back injuries. Triple highs or CHH days can be correlated with hernias.

Anderson's conclusions:

• There was a definite change in the individual during the so-called 'caution' days.

• The individual himself was unaware of this and could not understand why the accident happened.

• Caution days were identified by varying physical capabilities, mental capacity, and individual mood.

Germany: By 1954 a number of surveys had gathered momentum, after that of agricultural workers done by Dr Reingold Buchow of Humboldt University, Berlin, and Dr Otto Tope, Head of the Environmental Sanitation Department, Hanover.

Japan: Dr Tatai noted in *Biorhythm for Health Design* that, 'A foreman at an industrial company in Hiroshima has reported good results from the use of colour badges on caution days meaning "Let's all be aware of each other's biorhythm conditions." Similar badges with different colours for caution days have been effectively employed by the Japanese electric power company.'

Biorhythms are big business, often combined with Zen, Yoga or Buddhism and autogenic training. Many large insurance companies use them to improve staff safety, and to give considerable reductions in insurance premiums to other companies that do the same.

A sporting chance

The sports in this chapter represent a wide range of activities and biorhythm connections. There are individual sports, like tennis or boxing, where you have an opponent(s). There are other competitive sports, such as golf, where the individual plays against his or her own past achievements, as well as against others. In team sports like football and ice hockey an individual may dominate from time to time, but it is the complex interlinking of the biorhythms of the manager, captain and every team member with each other that indicates compatibility and therefore success. It is a complicated assessment. I have found similarities in biorhythm patterns between general circumstances in similar types of sport, for example football and rugby, or tennis and boxing. I am sure there are many other links yet to be revealed.

The sports enthusiast can therefore draw his or her own conclusions, and adapt the concepts outlined to their sporting activities. I hope this will help to clarify why one team wins or loses when two teams seem to be technically well matched. It should also help individuals to avoid accidents in sporting activities.

How to avoid accidents

In general, you are most accident prone on the following days in this order:

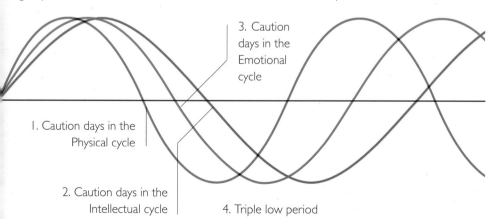

1. Caution days in the Physical cycle
2. Caution days in the Intellectual cycle
3. Caution days in the Emotional cycle
4. Triple low period
5. Triple high period if you are prone to over-exuberance

Physical caution days are associated with about eighty per cent of self-caused accidents, so it pays to:
• Be aware of such days and try to think positively.
• Consider taking Bach Remedies if you feel you might be vulnerable (page 109).
• Always prepare yourself thoroughly.

Golf

Golf is a game which requires skill on the physical and intellectual levels, as well as control of one's emotional reactions. To excel at a competitive level, even the best and most experienced players do better with at least two biorhythms in the high position.

Many professional golfers are aware of their biorhythms and a number of surveys have been done to illustrate the effect of biorhythms on a player's game. *Professional Golfer Magazine* (USA, 1970) revealed that 'of 44 major tournaments, 33 players won during high or rising biorhythm cycles'. A more detailed breakdown might have been of particular interest.

Aim to play during a triple high period, or, if life is not that convenient, choose a double high, preferably to include the Intellectual cycle. The inexperienced player would do best during a Physical and Intellectual high. For the experienced and already fit player, high Emotional and Intellectual cycles are just as good. The position of the Physical biorhythm seems to have a major impact on golfing errors.

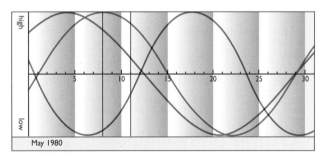

Case study: **Greg Norman, 8–11 May 1980**

Greg Norman, born on 10 February 1955, was ranked world number one in 1995. In 1980 he won the French Open at St Cloud by the largest margin in its history. He was high Emotionally and Intellectually (LHH).

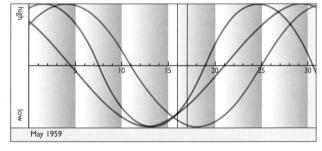

Case study: **Sam Snead, 16–17 May 1959**

Champion golfer, Snead, was born 27 May 1912. At the Sam Snead Festival, he scored the lowest thirty-six holes on record. Famous for his relaxed style, his personality and a familiar course overcame low biorhythms.

Horse riding

Horse riding will never be risk-free, even for the experienced and fit rider (*see Christopher Reeve chart, page 32*). I hope, though, that this section will help improve the odds in favour of the inexperienced rider, and perhaps even the experienced individual, be they show-jumper or jockey, who takes note of their biorhythms.

Riders should never be complacent, for riding is the third most dangerous sport (after water activities and motor sport).

In equestrian sports, the temperament and physical fitness of the horse has an effect on success or failure.

Inexperienced riders

From our research, we have reached some conclusions regarding the days on which inexperienced riders may fall from their horses:

• Physical caution days.

• Emotional caution days, generally accompanied by either a double high or a double low in the other biorhythms. In other words, these falls often occur on HCH or LCL days.

This leads us to assume that these accidents are usually connected with over-excitability or with extremely slow reactions.

• Riders who fall off and get straight back on again (unless seriously injured), generally fall off again, thus doubling the chance of personal injury and possible injury to the horse.

• Inexperienced riders should never ride on a public road, or on a horse they do not know and cannot handle with confidence.

Experienced riders

The most dangerous biorhythm combinations for experienced riders are:

• Triple lows. Numerous competitors at horse trials or other equestrian events have fallen while experiencing a triple low biorhythm phase. Many, very unfortunately, have been hurt.

• Caution days in the Physical cycle account for many falls, although this often results only in a dent to the rider's confidence.

• Occasionally caution days in the Emotional cycle are involved in falls from horses.

Safety tips for riders

• Always wear a protective helmet that meets national safety standards.

• Wear riding boots, that is boots with heels, never trainers. Without heels the foot can slip through the stirrup and get trapped if you fall.

• Check that all tack is fastened and comfortable.

• Do not wrap the reins around your fingers. If you fall, you may lose fingers.

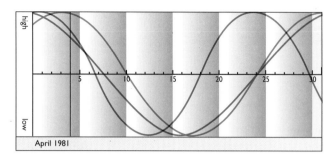

April 1981

Jockeys

The winning pattern

Given a reasonable mount, the best biorhythm patterns for a jockey are:

- Any two or all three cycles high.

Falls and accidents

Most falls to jockeys occur on:

- Triple lows or caution days in the Physical cycle.
- Occasionally, caution days in the Emotional cycle.

Case study: **Bob Champion,** *4 April 1981*

Bob Champion, born on 4 June 1948, had won numerous important races. On the day of the world famous Grand National steeplechase at Aintree, Liverpool, he was unwell.

Fortunately, his biorhythms were on a triple high (HHH) and he won the race. To verify the importance of jockeys' biorhythms, check the winners of any major race over a period of years.

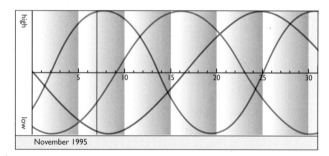

November 1995

Case study: **Damien Oliver,** *7 November 1995*

Damien Oliver was born on 22 June 1972. The Champion Jockey from Victoria, Australia, rode a ten-to-one outsider in the 1995 Melbourne Cup. He won the race. His biorhythms were HLL. He had a high Physical cycle giving him confidence, and a low Intellectual cycle providing good intuition.

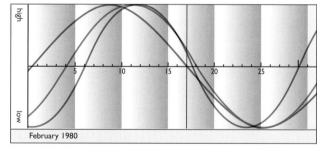

February 1980

Case study: **Yves St Martin,** *17 February 1980*

French jockey St Martin, born 8 September 1941, was heading for the start of a race at Durban. His horse bolted, and he fell and broke his left wrist. The horse was caught, ridden by local jockey Mark Sutherland and won. St Martin had both a Physical and an Intellectual caution day (CCH). The next day was an Emotional caution.

Boxing

In no other sport is the sportsman so totally alone and exposed as in a boxing ring, with only personal fitness, confidence and luck between him and possible serious injury.

There are visual records of boxing dating back to ancient Greece, but the first modern-day rules for the pitting of one man's strength against another's were drawn up by the Marquess of Queensbury, the Queensbury Rules of 1867.

In this aggressive sport, in which the aim is a knock out, the Physical biorhythm is most important, as in wrestling. Using biorhythms to choose the date of a match can affect the outcome. I once met British boxer Herel Graham who had won twenty-one fights, then lost the next one on points on a Intellectual caution day. This was interesting as it is usually sumo wrestling that requires more concentration.

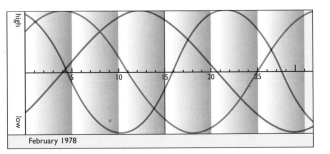

February 1978

Case study: **Muhammad Ali,** *15 February 1978*

Muhammad Ali was born on 17 January 1942. He fought Leon Spinks, born 11 July 1953, on 15 February 1978. Ali lost. Ali's biorhythms were LLH. Spinks' biorhythms were also LLH. In this case youth won. Both men had turned professional after winning Olympic gold medals as amateur heavyweight boxing champions.

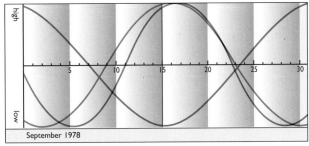

September 1978

Case study: **Muhammad Ali,** *15 September 1978*

Just 212 days after he had lost the WBA Heavyweight title to Leon Spinks *(left)*, Ali regained it, the only boxer to do so twice. This is still a record. Ali, with HHL, had the better biorhythms, Physically and Emotionally high. Spinks was LHL, with low Physical and Intellectual cycles. This fight attracted a record indoor crowd.

Men's tennis

Singles

Tennis is an individual sport in the same way that boxing, fencing, sumo wrestling, or even cycle racing are. One person is pitted against another: each stands or falls by a combination of their own efforts and skills, and some luck. However, for social creatures, being in a situation where there is little or no back up is rather unusual. This may be one of the many reasons why talented individuals with a good future ahead of them drop out from professional sport. It is also why the Physical cycle, which has as much to do with confidence as with physical strength and stamina, is crucial in these individual sports.

In sports which are orientated to a high degree of self-reliance, there seems to be evidence that high-level participants are able to compensate for a low Physical phase. These sportspersons appear to have perfected the technique of mind over matter.

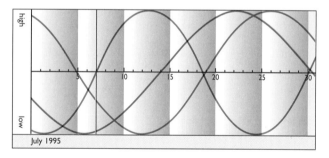

July 1995

Case study: **Andre Agassi, lost match, 7 July 1995**

Andre Agassi, born 29 April 1970, played in the semi-final at Wimbledon 1995 against Becker. Agassi's biorhythms were the worse of the two.

He was on a Physical caution day, his Emotional cycle was low and his Intellectual cycle was at its lowest (CLL). He lost the match.

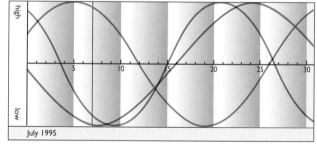

July 1995

Case study: **Boris Becker, won match, 7 July 1995**

Boris Becker, born on 22 November 1967, had two lows and a high Emotional biorhythm (LHL). The low Intellectual correlates with good intuition, and he won this semi-final. Although not good, his biorhythms were better than his opponent's.

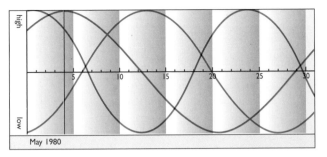

Case study: **Jimmy Connors, won match,** *4 May 1980*

Jimmy Connors was born on 2 September 1952. He beat John McEnroe in four sets in the final of the World Championship at Dallas, in spite of six-and-a-half year age difference that should have been to his disadvantage. Connors was making a successful come-back, prior to, and during, this period. His biorhythms then were HLH. *(See right for McEnroe's biorhythms in this match; and below for a later dramatic Conners' reversal.)*

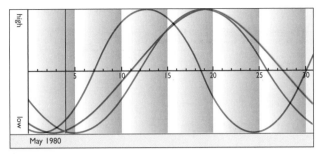

Case study: **John McEnroe, lost match,** *4 May 1980*

John McEnroe, born 16 February 1959, lost to Connors *(left)*. In Britain *The Guardian* reporter wrote: 'Has McEnroe declined so far that the result was irrelevant in assessing Connor's comeback?'

McEnroe admitted he had not got his act together. He was in a triple low (LLL), weakening his position against Connors' two highs and a low. *(See below for a later reversal of form, against a different opponent.)*

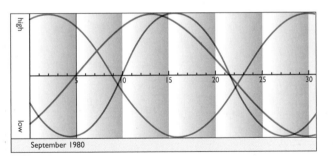

Case study: **Jimmy Connors, lost match,** *5 September 1980*

Jimmy Connors, then ranked third in the world, lost in the first round of the San Francisco Volvo Grand Prix to a then unknown student, Tim Mayotte, ranked 385th. Connors' biorhythms were LHC, Mayotte's HHH.

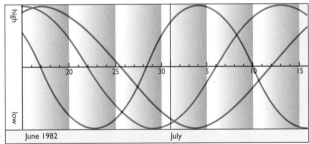

Case study: **John McEnroe, won match,** *I July 1982*

John McEnroe beat Tim Mayotte in straight sets in a semi-final at Wimbledon. McEnroe's biorhythms were HLL, Mayotte's were LLC.

This illustrates that a winning biorhythm can also be about comparison of individual circumstances: neither had stunning biorhythms.

Women's tennis

Singles

Women's singles tennis requires stamina, personality, elegance, strong nerves and resourcefulness.

Singles tennis pits woman against woman in a battle that can resemble gladiatorial combat, whereas in men's tennis, a fast serve can often win the day. In women's tennis, equally matched players are usually left to 'slug it out' on court.

The high degree of physicality required means that the Physical cycle is important. Where neither player has the advantage here, the other cycles then come into play.

Singles players should be self-reliant, and able to hold the attention of the crowd during a game which might last for some time. Practical knowledge of biorhythms is an advantage for professional or amateur sportspeople.

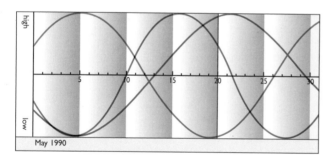

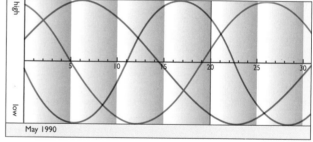

Case study: **Monica Seles, won match,** *20 May 1990*

Monica Seles was born on 2 December 1973. On 20 May 1990 she shocked the tennis world by beating Steffi Graf *(right)* in the German Open. Both had reasonable biorhythms, but Seles' HLH overcame Graf's HHL. The Intellectual cycle is important, as, when well-matched players meet, winning is often a case of mind over matter.

Case study: **Steffi Graf, lost match,** *20 May 1990*

Steffi Graf was born on 14 June 1969. She had not lost a match since the French Open final in 1989. Steffi Graf played Monica Seles *(left)*, a sixteen-year-old Yugoslav, and lost. Steffi Graf's biorhythms were HHL. Usually a low Intellectual biorhythm means high intuition, but under stress or pressure this may not always happen.

Doubles

Too compatible?

Martina Navratilova and Chris Evert are biorhythmically 100 per cent compatible in the Physical cycle, so neither player had the physical edge over the other. When they met as opponents, the tennis was memorable, but anyone can only be in their high phases for about half the time. When both players were Physically down, or experiencing a caution day at the same time, their partnership would be very vulnerable. Emotionally they are

64 per cent compatible, and Intellectually, 58 per cent, so one player would always have a high Intellectual phase when the other was more intuitive. Perhaps this is why we did not hear more of a Lloyd/Navratilova partnership. Another aspect could lie in their 100 per cent Physical compatibility which can create rivalry.

Compatible

A compatible partnership in sport or work is usually reflected in success. It is best if all three cycles are over fifty per cent, with no single one too highly matched.

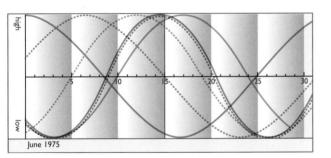

Case study: **Lloyd and Navratilova**, *15 June 1975*

Occasional doubles partners Chris Evert, born 21 December 1954, and Martina Navratilova, born 18 October 1956, won the French Open in 1975. Lloyd's biorhythms *(unbroken lines on chart)* were HHL, Navratilova's *(broken lines on chart)* were HHC. On this occasion, four highs overcame other incompatibilities.

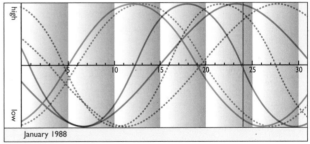

Case study: **Turnbull and Lloyd**, *24 January 1988*

Wendy Turnbull, born on 26 November 1952, and Chris Evert were a successful doubles partnership. Their excellent compatibility is Physical 65 per cent, Emotional 57, and Intellectual 82. They won the Australian Open in 1988. Turnbull's biorhythms *(broken lines on chart)* were HLH, Evert's *(unbroken lines on chart)* CLH.

Ice hockey

Ice hockey is a team game, yet one in which individuals often stand out or take the lead, making an additional impact by inspiring the whole team. Ideally, within any sports team, the compatibility of players should range from forty per cent to seventy per cent. Those working most closely together should be more Physically compatible with members of their sub-group. The bottom line of team compatibility is gen-erally regarded as thirty-nine per cent Physical compatibility. Happily, in a team sport the Physical low of an individual can be compensated for by high cycles of other team members.

When a fight breaks out during a game, it is likely that the biorhythms of the two opposing players initially involved are clashing. (*See football examples on pages 97–98.*) Calculating team biorhythms is a complex but worthwhile study.

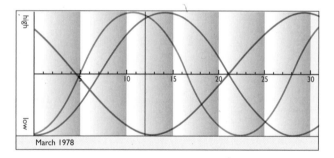

March 1978

Case study: **Bobby Hull**, *12 March 1978*

Bobby Hull was born on 3 January 1939. He scored his 1,000th goal in his 1,600th game. His biorhythms were HHL, a perfect sequence for success in sporting activities.

The Intellectual cycle is important in professional sport. When low, the Intellectual biorhythm gives high intuition, reflected here in scoring accuracy.

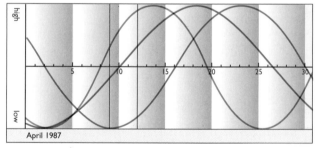

April 1987

Case study: **Wayne Gretzky, 9, 12 April 1987**

Another Hockey Hall of Fame Canadian, Wayne Gretzky, was born on 26 January 1961. The game's greatest scorer has broken more records than any other player. On 9 April (HLL) he had the most assists in a single play-off game. On the 12th (HLH) he scored the most points in one period in a single play-off game.

Figure skating

In pairs figure skating, excellent biorhythm compatibility and a high level of trust are paramount for success. The man and woman must be responsive to one another and move as one with exceptional grace, skill and fine coordination of movement.

In pairs ice dancing, the Emotional cycle is important, because of the creativity expressed through the choreography, costumes and the trust the woman must have in her partner during throws and numerous complicated movements.

Unlike most other sports pairs, genuine enjoyment must exist, and be reflected in the faces and movements of winning pairs.

The Physical biorhythm provides the stamina. The Intellectual biorhythm is significant because of the detailed skating programmes, which must be perfectly remembered and coordinated by both.

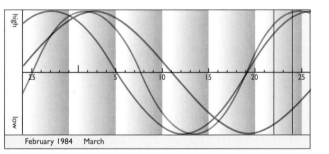

Case study: **Jayne Torvill, *22–24 March 1984***

Jayne Torvill was born on 7 October 1957. In February, Jayne Torvill and Christopher Dean won Olympic gold with a perfect set of nine sixes. In March at the World Ice Dance Championship in Ottawa, they received the highest tally ever (twenty-nine) maximum six marks. Torvill was HHL during this period.

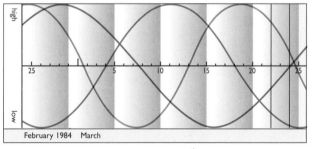

Case study: **Christopher Dean, *22–24 March 1984***

Christopher Dean was born on 27 July 1958. In March at the World Ice Dance Championship in Ottawa, Dean, the stronger of the two, was HLL on the 22nd and CLC by the 24th. The biorhythm compatibility of Jayne Torvill and Christopher Dean is Physical 48 per cent, Emotional 7 per cent and Intellectual 76 per cent.

95

Men's skiing

Women's skiing

Men's alpine skiing is a dramatic sport that requires immense physical fitness, confidence and coordination.

The position of the Physical biorhythm is crucial to success for it gives the stamina for speed, the confidence to take swift action, and the coordination to prevent injury and maximize self-reliance.

The Intellectual cycle is of next importance in this thrilling and demanding sport.

Although women's alpine skiing is slower than men's, participants must still be physically fit and thrive on a challenge. Like mountaineers, many alpine skiiers can become obsessive. To prevent this, and to assess complicated terrain and obstacles, the Intellectual biorhythm is important. Alpine skiing provides more scope for challenges than for creativity, but there is a high risk of accidents in all such sports.

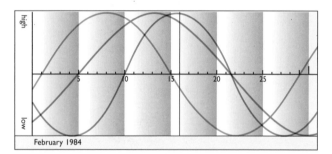

February 1984

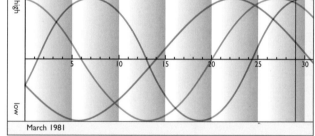

March 1981

Case study: **William D. Johnson,** *16 February 1984*

American William Johnson was born in Sarajevo, Yugoslavia, on 30 March 1960. In the 1984 Olympics at Sarajevo, he achieved the highest average speed in the Olympic downhill race, 104.53 kilometres per hour (64.95 mph). His biorhythms were HLH. The Emotional low was probably calming in front of a home crowd.

Case study: **Tiina Lehtola,** *29 March 1981*

Tiina Lehtola was born in Finland on 3 August 1962. She achieved the women's record for the longest ski jump, 110 metres (361 feet), on 29 March 1981 at Ruka, Finland. Her biorhythms on the day were HHH. This biorhythm combination, when directed at a specific goal, helps fortify and maximize natural talent.

Football

Biorhythm compatibility in a football team

Teams must work as a whole, and to achieve this there should be balance. It would not be good, for instance, if everyone had high or low biorhythms at the same time. Such patterns would produce confusion in the team's form, and create individual rivalry. Performance might be wonderful if everyone had high biorhythms, but when the lows came the team would be knocked out of competition.

Effect of highs

Players on triple highs may clash during a game due to over-exuberance. Players coming out of a triple high often act temperamentally, especially if under pressure.

Effect of caution days

Possible dramatic effects of caution days within opposing teams, which could apply to any sport, are illustrated by incidents like the one in the English match between Arsenal and Manchester United on 20 October 1990. There was an exceptionally ugly incident involving twenty-one players. The London-based *Sunday Telegraph* reported that Nigel Winterburn and Anders Limpar of Arsenal and Dennis Irwin and Paul Ince of Manchester United were the first players involved.

Their biorhythms (*see page 98*) showed that Irwin and Ince were both experiencing caution days in the Emotional cycle and that Winterburn and (again) Irwin had caution days in the Physical cycle. Limpar had an Intellectual caution day. The odds against all four players involved in one incident all having caution days on the same day is about 140 to one. Also, Alex Ferguson, then the manager of Manchester United, was on a Physical caution day.

During a separate incident on the same day, in the game between Manchester City and Derby County, Adrian Heath was sent off in extra time. He was experiencing a caution day in the Intellectual cycle.

If the players had been aware of their biorhythms, they might have been able to maintain self-control.

Effect of lows

In the match quoted, Manager of Arsenal, George Graham, was experiencing triple low biorhythms. These are generally associated with dulled responses.

Future research

After the Arsenal versus Manchester United match, the London Biorhythm Company attempted, unsuccessfully, to get British football clubs to use biorhythms. We can provide additional information to anyone interested.

Game: Arsenal versus Manchester United, *20 October 1990*

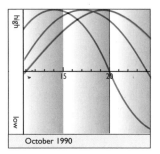

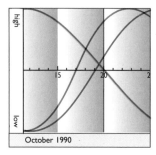

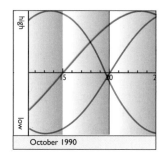

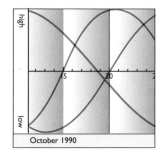

Case study:
**Nigel Winterburn,
Arsenal**

Nigel Winterburn, born
11 December 1963, had a
Physical caution day (CHH),
leaving an HHH; this could
equal aggression.

Case study:
**Anders Limpar,
Arsenal**

Anders Limpar was born on
24 September 1965. He was
experiencing an Intellectual
caution day (HHC) following
a triple high.

Case study:
**Denis Irwin,
Manchester United**

Denis Irwin was born on 31
July 1965. On the day of the
match he was on a double
caution day, Physical and
Emotional (CCH).

Case study:
**Paul Ince,
Manchester United**

Paul Ince was born on 21
October 1967. He was on
an Emotional caution day
(HCL). Remember,
forewarned is forearmed.

Dismissals

On 11 January 1991, *The Times* (London) published a list
of dismissals of football league players so far that season,
a total of 132, including five players listed twice.

We analyzed the players' biorhythms. There were:
- Over twice as many dismissals on caution days in the
Physical cycle than would be expected by chance.
- More than double the dismissals on caution days in
the Intellectual cycle than chance would predict.
- No major link with the Emotional cycle.
- Nearly twice as many non-caution day dismissals dur-
ing Intellectual highs compared to Intellectual lows.

Of seventeen of the younger players involved in incidents, twelve occurred on caution days in the
Intellectual cycle and three on other caution days. The
last two young players listed were in triple low phases.

Although the total sample of players is numerically
small, it does seem that self-control (on the football
field) is related to the Intellectual cycle. Additionally,
this self-control seems to increase with maturity and
therefore can be learnt.

Referees' dates of birth were not available, so we
were unable to work out their biorhythms, which I
believe would have been both interesting and significant. It is not only players who can be in the wrong.

American football

One of the most apparently successful biorhythm prediction methods was developed by Nancy Roberts and Michael Wallerstein in the 1970s for use in American football prediction. They outlined their results in a paper entitled 'All Together on the Bio-Curve', published in *Human Behavior*, April 1973.

They have never divulged exactly how they did their calculations, but they did apparently achieve a ninety per cent success rate in predicting the winning teams. Here is a summary of some of the methods they used:

• They placed a heavier weight on the biorhythms of the team leaders and the coach.

• They decided that a player with very good biorhythms would not contribute to the overall team effort, as they felt that he would be likely to play his own game.

• A player with mediocre biorhythms is much more likely to be cooperative during the game.

They totalled points for each player, and adjusted a player's biorhythm score by downgrading the very good biorhythms and upgrading the mediocre ones. Biorhythms they considered to be average were not adjusted. If the player had exhausted himself recently, they downgraded any peaks. Similarly, if the player had just returned from a relaxing holiday any troughs would be upgraded. A number of other biorhythm experts did not agree with their research or their assumptions, but it does appear that they were very successful in their predictions as applied to team work in American football.

Case study: **Tony Dorsett, *3 January 1983***

American Tony Dorsett was born on 7 April 1954. He held several records. Dorsett joined the Dallas Cowboys in 1977. Playing for the Dallas Cowboys in a game against the Minnesota Vikings, he achieved the longest ever run from scrimmage and scored a touchdown. The record run was 90.5 metres (99 yards). Tony Dorsett's biorhythms on 3 January 1983 were HLH.

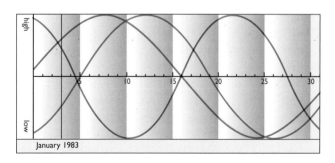

January 1983

The discovery of biorhythms

Greek doctors of the third and fourth centuries BC, and North African physicians of 1,000 years ago, took account of the physical cycles of their patients during treatment. Yet biorhythms as we know them today were not recorded until the turn of the twentieth century.

Between 1890 and 1905 Dr Wilhelm Fliess (1859–1928), a prominent ear, nose and throat specialist, recorded and analyzed the medical records of several thousand of his patients. This original research concentrated mainly on middle-class children and their mothers, because these formed the majority of his patients. From this study he discovered the existence of a Physical cycle governing births, deaths, and immunity to and recovery from illness, and an Emotional cycle governing the mothers' reactions to these events. Fliess worked through over 10,000 family trees for three generations to verify that the two biorhythm cycles existed.

Once he was satisfied that they did, he published a number of books, papers and pamphlets on the subject. These caught public enthusiasm, and for some years biorhythm cycles were very popular within the German-speaking world, then the centre of medical advances. At this time there was also great interest in the origins of mankind, anthropology and mysticism. These were the fashionable subjects of intellectual debate.

Fliess was a close friend and colleague of the pioneer of psychoanalysis, Sigmund Freud (1856–1939). He wrote to congratulate Fliess on 'this major breakthrough in biology' after Fliess explained his initial findings.

Freud then carried out analytical tests which confirmed many of Fliess' theories. They worked together for many years – until they quarrelled, violently. This was probably because Fliess believed Freud had discussed Fliess' theories with one of his acquaintances, Hermann Swoboda, who later published Fliess' biorhythm work under his own name. They also argued about bisexuality.

Freud used dream analysis to confirm the existence of the Emotional biorhythm cycle, and today, in France in particular, biorhythms are used to enhance the effectiveness of conventional treatment in this area.

When Fliess began his research, the theory of bisexuality was another fashionable subject of discussion. This was probably why Fliess chose to link sexuality and biorhythms, which he did by referring to the Physical cycle as the male cycle, and the Emotional cycle (he always called it the 'Sensitivity' cycle, a name which stuck until the 1960s) as the female cycle. At that time, intellectuals were fascinated with the early results of psychoanalysis, and the study of biorhythms probably began as an off-shoot of this interest.

Hermann Swoboda, the likely cause of the split between Fliess and Freud, was later to become Professor of Psychology at the University of Vienna. Here he had begun his own research, and, in 1951, the City of Vienna awarded him a special honorary medal for his life's work in the study of the rhythms of life.

In 1945, Hermann Swoboda had had the misfortune to watch his original research papers being confiscated

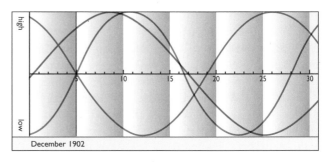

Dr Sigmund Freud *(left)*, pioneer of psychoanalysis, and Dr Wilhelm Fliess *(right)*, who observed the first biorhythm cycles. The friends were photographed in about 1890.

Case study: **Wilhelm Fliess**, *5 December 1902*

Fliess was born on 24 October 1859. Around 5 December (CCH), an unhappy Fliess wrote to Freud after a long gap. This sealed a fermenting quarrel.

The partnership between Fliess and Freud is a fascinating study. Fliess, the introvert, was intellectually more rigorous, while extrovert Freud was able to put many of their ideas to use. Their Physical compatibility was 91 per cent (competitive), Emotional 51 per cent and Intellectual 27 per cent (when one was intuitive, the other was practical). After they quarrelled, Fliess sank into a workaholic depression, while Freud's fame increased. It is believed that without the stimulation of their partnership, neither man would have achieved success to the same degree.

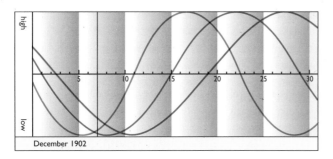

Case study: **Sigmund Freud**, *7 December 1902*

Freud was born on 6 May 1856. His biorhythms were LLL on the day he responded curtly to Fliess. Fliess' daughter had been stillborn.

Hermann Swoboda (1873–1963) was awarded an honorary medal by the City of Vienna for his work on biorhythms.

by Russian troops who had occupied Vienna at the end of the Second World War. Until his death in 1963, he still believed that the research was lost forever, but it now seems that it was not. The research papers were taken to Moscow, where they remained unopened until about 1959 when they were sent to East Germany (*see page 105*).

In the 1930s there was an awakening of interest in biorhythms in the United States and Canada, and a famous study which was to become known as the Hersey Railway Study was undertaken (*see page 20*).

Intellectual cycle

In the 1920s, Alfred Teltscher, a Professor of Engineering at the University of Innsbrück, Austria, observed and recorded the Intellectual biorhythm cycle.

Teltscher had begun to wonder why the performance of individuals varied so dramatically from day to day: even his brightest students could behave stupidly. He kept daily records of their performances, and from them he was able to suggest that an Intellectual cycle existed in humans. This cycle has now been confirmed, as has its relationship to the secretions of the thyroid and other glands. Generally, it is not clinically observable before the onset of puberty.

Biorhythm gadgets

In the 1930s, Alfred Judt, an engineer from Bremen, North Germany, devised tables for calculating biorhythms, including the Intellectual cycle. This is the first recorded calculation aid, although Hermann Swoboda had earlier designed a slide rule which showed caution days in the Physical and Emotional biorhythms. Swiss engineer Hans Frueh made the first biorhythm calculating machine, and Certina of Switzerland followed with the first biorhythm watch, manufactured continuously until the 1970s.

In 1980 The London Biorhythm Company developed the biorhythm wheel to display biorhythms.

Modern developments

After the Second World War, the study and application of biorhythms to everyday life, including work and relationships, came into its own.

From the 1940s to the 1960s
1945: More widespread acceptance of biorhythms began when *Reader's Digest* in the USA printed one of the first popular articles on the subject. This was partly based on the Hersey Railway Study *(see page 20).*

1950s to 1960s: George Thommen, an entrepreneur from Switzerland, introduced biorhythms to the US public. He later joined forces with Bernard Gittelson, who wrote a best-selling paperback on the subject. For some years they edited an international biorhythm newsletter.

1953: During the Korean War, Dr Philippe A. Costin, later to become Director of Medical Services for the Canadian Armed Forces, began to collect statistics on biorhythms. Much of his research was related to military cases. Four out of five deaths during military action occurred on caution days in the Physical cycle. *(For an early military example, see the chart of King Richard the Lionheart, opposite.)* Dr Costin became founder and later a Chairman of The International Biorhythm Association. For over thirty years he has continued studying the subject.

Popularizing biorhythms led to the Kitchener (Ontario) Bus Company reducing its accident rate by sixty per cent when biorhythms were used. Companies such as Gulf Canada also took them on board.

1960s: The study of biorhythms increased. They became widely accepted in Japan and other Pacific countries.

The study of biorhythms was taken to Japan by Professor Kichinosuke Tatai, MD, who had learned about them while studying for his second degree at the Harvard School for Public Health. He was so impressed with the the positive results he had read that he set up the Japan Biorhythm Laboratory (JBL) in Tokyo.

Since then hundreds of studies have been carried out in Japan, including those to help increase productivity in the workplace by using biorhythm compatibility; and those to prevent industrial and motor accidents, using the 'forewarned is forearmed' principle.

As the use of biorhythms became more popular in Japan, accident rates — both motoring and industrial — decreased. In some cases this reduction was by as much as eighty per cent. Major insurance companies obviously became interested because it saved them claims. Some of these savings were passed on in reduced premiums, others were used for biorhythm research, which proliferated. This increased the potential of biorhythms, and they were combined with autogenic training at the JBL and re-exported, back (again) to Europe via the USA.

So, biorhythms had become linked with autogenic training, a link I personally dislike because I believe it destroys originality, although I do concede it works very effectively in the way intended. I have to say, and it is a personal opinion, that linking the two disciplines hints at brainwashing; this might be a cultural difference.

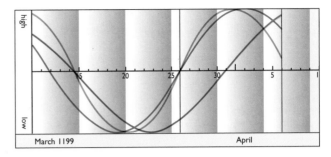

March 1199   April

Case study: **Richard I, 'Richard the Lionheart',**
26 March, 6 April 1199

1961: The original Swoboda research papers had been taken to Moscow where they remained unopened until about 1959. They were then sent to East Berlin to be translated. By 1961 the East German authorities became very interested in the subject of biorhythms and a number of theses on biorhythms were published. I am told that these original research papers still exist in the old Stazi headquarters in Berlin. Perhaps one day they will be openly published or returned to Austria.

From East Germany, knowledge of biorhythms filtered throughout Eastern Europe. In Western Europe, life was becoming increasingly influenced by ancient Asian philosophies. The Beatles travelled to India in their search for personal growth. The hippy trail and communing with nature became fashionable. The resurgence of biorhythms slotted neatly into that era.

Biorhythms were popular, but there was a deliberate policy by 'the Establishment' to shut them out. Medical friends were pilloried by the hierarchy and, to a lesser extent, by the scientific establishment. Times, thank goodness, have changed. There is now a British Medical Association reference point on biorhythms – me.

1965: A study by German policeman Max Steves was published in the national police journal and widely publicized in popular magazines. He analyzed the biorhythms for 1,200 drivers involved in road accidents. He found that 648 (54 per cent) occurred on caution days; also, twice as many of the remaining incidents occurred when the biorhythms were low, than when they were high.

Richard I, King of England and of some French territories, was born 8 September 1157. He was the third son of Henry II and Eleanor of Poitou. In 1189 he succeeded to the English throne, and inherited some French properties. As well as going to The Crusades, he led numerous campaigns on 'French' soil to subdue noblemen rebelling against his authority. While trying to break the seige of the Castle of Châlus, he made a headstrong charge towards the town walls without covering himself properly and was wounded in the shoulder by an arrow. As in most modern military accidents, this happened on a caution day in the Physical cycle (CCL). He died on his next Physical caution day (CHH).

I believe this example to be the earliest historical biorhythm yet charted. To complete it, I first had to absorb the intricacies of the French medieval calendar.

This biorhythm pattern also figures largely in motorcycle accidents where unnecessary risks are taken. This is particularly true of young people who rush to overtake when this cannot be done safely.

To bring us up to date, when Prime Minister John Major challenged himself in 1995 for leadership of Conservative Party, his biorhythms were almost identical to those of Richard I, illustrated above (CHH).

From the 1970s to the 1990s

1970s: Many research studies, some reporting favourably, some not, were undertaken, most particularly in the USA. There in 1973, Professor Harold R. Willis and colleagues at Missouri Southern State College linked the Physical biorhythm to the human autonomic nervous system (which governs our speed of reaction).

Studies, undertaken at the US Naval Postgraduate School in Monterey, California, verified much of the work in the field of biorhythm research. Dr Douglas E. Neil has written a number of papers on his research, and copies of these are generally available. His position enabled him to use the Fast Fourier Transform (FFT) to analyze the results of his research, which are mainly pro-biorhythm. In 1976 the FFT was at the forefront of computer technology.

1978: The USSR announced that the authorities were interested in biorhythm research. Associated Press quoted *Pravda*, the official State newspaper, as the source of a report that a study of 5,000 taxi drivers was being carried out in connection with biorhythm research, but no results of this study have been made available.

1979: *The (London) Evening News* and the Greater London Council undertook a large study on the connection between motor accidents and biorhythms.

Nottingham County Council undertook a broadly similar study on 50,000 volunteer car drivers, who each kept a personal record for one month. Researchers then collated these. The results became available some seven years later, and the conclusions were generally in favour of biorhythms.

1980: The London Biorhythm Company was formed, and an International Newsletter began in 1983.

1981: *The Nursing Times*, London, published two full-length feature articles on biorhythms, written under a pseudonym by a highly qualified doctor.

1980s: The study of biorhythms was incorporated into the course work for psychology degrees at some British universities. This number is increasing.

1983: The first major studies carried out by The London Biorhythm Company concerned the Irish hunger strikers. An abbreviated version of the study was published in *The Vegetarian*. The full version is available on request.

1989: In Athens at the Sixteenth World Congress of Complementary Medicine, it was reported that studies on biorhythms at PhD level were being undertaken in many countries. I met an expert on biorhythms from isolated Romania, which rather surprised me. A Hungarian, now living in Australia, confirmed that, as a former worker in the nuclear industry, she had been scheduled, according to her biorhythms, to avoid having to work in high risk areas on caution days.

1990s: Biorhythms are taught and used in many top hospitals in Britain.

1993: The London Biorhythm Company did a study on deaths in prisons in England and Wales with a view to promoting the use of biorhythms in suicide prevention. Many unnecessary tragedies could then be avoided.

Today

In Japan biorhythms are now firmly established as part of the culture. Major insurance companies, airlines, transport companies, large industrial firms, and even the police, teach their staff to be aware of caution days. Some insurance companies even distribute biorhythm charts free as part of their 'social policy'.

The Germans and the Swiss continue with biorhythm research and try to apply their findings.

In the USA, United Airlines and others have an expanding programme of using biorhythms to assess personnel. Other major companies are researching and utilizing the cycles to help reduce accidents and improve performance. Sports psychology and biorhythms is a fast expanding field of research.

Methods of calculation

The biorhythm wheel

The wheel in *The Biorhythm Kit* is the easiest and most dependable way of calculating biorhythms. It can be used for any person, for any year. If you ever wish to verify this, use the mathematical calculation below.

Mathematical calculation

This is useful to help you understand the basis of biorhythms, or if you want to double-check a calculation. **Method**: Take the number of complete years lived. Multiply this by 365 (days). Add one day for each leap year lived (*see Leap year table, page 25*). Count the number of extra days in the current year, including the day you are calculating for. Divide this total by the number of days in each cycle in turn: twenty-three days for the Physical; twenty-eight days for the Emotional; and thirty-three days for the Intellectual. If you wish, you can chart your biorhythms each day on graph paper.

Computers and biorhythms

Both life and biorhythms are now dependent on computers. Programs are available, but are they accurate? In 1992 a graduate at the University of Ulster, Northern Ireland, conducted an independent survey of commercially available programs. This showed that three of the five programs tested were inaccurate – some even displayed apparently random numbers. Also, many computer programs, and specialized calculators in particular, currently only accept dates between 1900 and 1999.

Conclusion

The acceptance of biorhythms has come a long way in 100 years. Their potential for improving our lives is being realized, as we become more in tune with ourselves and others. In every life there are good days and bad days; active days and quiet days. Using biorhythms can help us to relax and enjoy the restful times; to understand and plan for the difficult times; and to concentrate on success in the good times to come.

The London Biorhythm Company

In 1980 I founded The London Biorhythm Company. This independent organization is the British Medical Association reference point for information on biorhythms. One of the main objectives of the company is to gather evidence to prove the accuracy of biorhythms in reflecting the patterns of behaviour in our lives. The organization also sells various original biorhythm products with European translations.

Our collection of letters and questionnaires is almost certainly the largest source of such information on biorhythms anywhere in the world. All the letters we receive are read, categorized, calculated to find the biorhythms and filed for future reference. Each case helps us to understand biorhythm patterns and the way they affect us all. Many of these effects are explained in this book. Others you will need to consider for yourself, using the principles outlined. We cannot cover every eventuality and your interpretation of biorhythms needs to contain an element of common sense.

After you have read this book, you might want to write to us. We are always pleased to receive your impressions or details of incidents you find interesting. There is a questionnaire we can send, on which you can recount the circumstances of an incident you think may be related to biorhythms. It is a guide to the information we are looking for, but do write about anything that you feel is relevant. Remember when writing that we need the date of birth of the person involved and the exact date of the incident.

We try to reply to everyone, and sometimes we can offer help or advice. The returned questionnaires show a much higher ratio of caution-day accidents than most other research, but ours is a self-selected group.

Ongoing research

We have undertaken a major study on biorhythm research and suicides. We are cooperating with the Institut für Gerichtliche Medizin der Universität Innsbruck (Centre for Forensic Medicine, University of Innsbruck).

Areas of particular interest are vaccine damage and innoculation reactions; Brief Recurrent Depression (BRD); and tinnitus (the hearing abnormality).

Another developing interest is adverse reactions from domestic animals – incidents like dog bites from friendly dogs. I am now convinced that animals can sense changes in our moods, and can thus 'pick up' on our caution days. We are working on a project with the post office, who are supplying incident figures in bulk.

The London Biorhythm Company supplies a range of biorhythm products. Please write, enclosing a stamped, self-addressed envelope, for a free chart and explanation, or a questionnaire, or details of products or a price list. We also give talks to groups by arrangement.

UK: Biorhythms, PO Box 8390, South Kensington, London SW7 2PT. **Eire:** PO Box 84, Wexford City, Wexford. **South Africa**: PO Box 47384, Parklands 2121, Johannesburg. **India:** 303 Banjara Bhavan, Banjara Hills Road 1, Hyderabad 500 034.

The author

Jacyntha Crawley has studied biorhythms for many years, initially as a hobby. In 1980 she founded The London Biorhythm Company. Looking back now, she realizes that this was an HLH period and that the idea came to her on an HLC day. The intention was to undertake rigorous analysis in the field of biorhythm research, and to make biorhythm-related products available to the public. Since then she has pioneered new research into the subject, and devised the biorhythm wheel to make the calculation of biorhythms easier. For this, the company was awarded a DTI Enterprise Initiative grant.

Over the years she has appeared on local and national radio stations in the UK, where she has also made TV appearances. She contributed to *The Reader's Digest Dictionary of Alternative Medicine*, which has been widely translated.

Her work has featured in a number of magazines and newspapers in several countries.

Jacyntha's interests are wide-ranging, from various forms of alternative medicine, to human rights and the promotion of open and responsible government. She helped set up the charity Age-Link, as an off-shoot of the London InterVarsity Club's (IVC) Community Service Section, which she had founded.

She has initiated, usually by accident, GLUG, a recycling programme, a shared car scheme and a voluntarily run cafeteria at IVC called Burnt Offerings.

Practical conservation is a hands-on interest, which has included deconstructing a London Docklands sail loft for re-erection in a museum. She has worked voluntarily in Guernsey, the Hebrides, and on Fair Isle, to connect the first windmill to produce domestic electricity. She lives in Surrey where she is involved in community projects.

Information and addresses

Dr Bach's Flower Remedies. Rescue Remedy is suitable to soothe the effects of any combination of caution days or biorhythm lows. Other recommended Bach combinations are Cerato and Clematis for Physical caution days; Aspen and Gentian for Emotional caution days; White Chestnut and Wild Oat for Intellectual caution days. These have no adverse effects.
Flower Essence Society. PO Box 459, Nevada City, CA 95959.
Depression Hotline. Tel: (800) 551-0008. Please consult your local telephone directory for counselling services in your area.
Freud Museum. Bookshop. 20 Maresfield Gardens, London NW3 5SX, UK.
National Health Information Center. PO Box 1133, Washington, DC 20013-1133, Tel: (800) 336-4797.
American Health Foundation. 320 East 43rd Street, New York, NY 10017. Tel: (212) 953-1900.
The American Holistic Medical Association. 4101 Lake Boon Trail, Suite 201, Raleigh, NC 27607. Tel: (919) 787-5181.
American Institute for Preventative Medicine. 24450 Evergreen Road, Southfield, MI 48075. Tel: (313) 352-7666.
Research Centre into Bioenergetics. Advice and research. 11 rue Lafayette, Paris F75009, France.
The Society of Metaphysicians Limited. Collection of historic biorhythm gadgets. Visitors by appointment. General product/book list. Hastings, East Sussex, TN35 4PG, UK.

Selected reading

Anderson, R. K. 'Biorhythm – Man's Timing Mechanism'. Park Ridge, Illinois, American Society of Safety Engineers, 1972.

Aschoff, J. 'Circadian Systems in Man and Their Implications', *Hospital Practice*, May 1976, pp. 51–70.

Bennet, G. *Beyond Endurance. Survival at the Extremes*. London, Secker and Warburg, 1983.

Brady, T. 'Biorhythm What?' *TAC ATTACK*, Langley, West Virginia, Langley Air Force Base, March 1972.

Biological Rhythms in Psychiatry and Medicine. Department of Health and Education Welfare, National Institute of Mental Health, 5600 Fishers Lane, Rockville, Maryland 20852. Covers most human cycles. Copy free on request.

Caravias-Graas, N. *The Calendar*. Originally published in German (*Der Kalendar*), 1920s. Athens, 1977. Now in English, French, German, Greek and Spanish. Available from The London Biorhythm Company.

Case, J. 'Predictive Powers in Biorhythm Analysis in the Performance of Football Players'. Joplin, Missouri, Missouri State Southern College, 1972.

Cooper, W. and Smith, T. *Human Potential*. Newton Abbot, Devon, David and Charles, 1981.

Eating Behaviour: Preferences, Consumption Patterns and Biorhythms. Natick, Massachusetts, USA. US Army Research and Development, Food Sciences Laboratories Technical Report (contract DAAK03–74–c–0233). 1978.

Freud, S. *The Complete Letters of Sigmund Freud to Wilhelm Fliess, 1887–1904*. Trans. by J. Moussault-Masson. Cambridge, Mass., Harvard University Press, 1988.

Gardner, M. *Mathematical Carnival*. London, Penguin, 1975. Anti-Fliess.

Gatty, Ronald. *The Body Clock Diet*. New York, Simon & Schuster; London, Victor Golancz, 1978; paperback 1982.

Gross, H. M. *Biorhythms*. Originally published in Germany. English trans. Albuquerque, New Mexico, Motivation Development Center, 1975.

Halberg, F. 'Implications of Biological Rhythms for Clinical Practice', *Hospital Practice*, January 1977, pp. 139–49.

Johnson, C. *Fasting, Longevity and Immortality*. From Survival, Turkey Hills, Haddam, Connecticut 06438, or from The London Biorhythm Company.

Journal of Interdisciplinary Cycle Research. Amsterdam, the Netherlands, Elsevir. Quarterly.

Lagrifa, M. *Connaissez vos Biorythmes pour reussir*. Paris, Editions de Vecchi, 1989. (French edition only.)

Luce, G. G. *Biological Rhythms in the Human and Animal Physiology*. New York, Dover, 1971. Written by a leading expert, this book is a classic study.

Luce, G. G. *Bodytime: Psychological Rhythms and Social Stress*. New York, Pantheon, 1971. Informative and entertaining.

McKenna, F. P. 'The human factor in driving accidents. An overview of approaches and problems.' Cambridge University, Applied Psychology Unit, CB2 2BF. Anti-biorhythms research. Copy on request.

Neil, D., Giannotti, L. and Wyatt, T. 'Statistical Analysis of the Theory of Biorhythms'. Monterey, California, Naval Postgraduate School (unpublished). Copy on request.

Nelson, D. J. and Colville, D. H. *Life Force in the Great Pyramids*. Marina Del Ray, California, De Vorss and Company, 1977. Chapters on biorythms.

Palmer, P. 'The effect of biorhythms on road accidents'. Crowthorne, Berkshire, UK Department of Transport, 1979. An anti-biorhythms study. Copy on request.

Ruperti, A. *Cycles of Becoming. The Planetary Pattern of Growth*. Reno, Nevada, CRCS, 1978.

Saltarini, H. *Bioritmo*. Milan, SIAD Edizioni, 1977. (Italian edition only.)

Swain, A. D., Altman, J. W. and Rock, L. W. Jr. 'Human Error Qualification'. Albuquerque, New Mexico, Sandia Corporation, 1963.

Tatai, Professor Kichinosuke. *Biorhythms for Living*. Tokyo, Japan Corporation, Inc., 1977. Founder of the Japanese Biorhythm Association.

Tatai, Professor Kichinosuke. *Biorhythm for Health Design*. Tokyo, Japan Corporation, Inc., 1977. Introduces autogenic training techniques.

Thommen, G. S. *Is This Your Day?* New York, Crown, 1973.

Tittmar, H. G., supervisor of various theses. Department of Psychology, University of Ulster, Northern Ireland. Copies on request. Uses biorhythms as a sports psychologist up to Olympic level.

Tope, O. *Biorhythmishe Einflusse und ihre Auswirkung in Fuhrparkbetrieben*. Hannover, Germany, Sonderdruck: Staedtehygiene 9/1956.

Willis, H. R. 'Biorhythms and Its Relationship to Human Error'. Proc. of the Sixteenth Annual Meeting of the Human Factors Society. Santa Monica, California, 1972.

von Durckheim, K. G. *Hara – The Vital Centre of Man*. London, Unwin, 1977.

Index

Picture credits

We have made every effort to trace and acknowledge the copyright holders of the photographs used in this book as listed below. We apologise for any inadvertent omissions and invite copyright holders to contact Eddison Sadd direct.

The Bridgeman Art Library/Courtauld Institute Galleries 58; Camera Press 44, 50, 51; Liz Eddison 22, 63, 73; Mary Evans 48, 102; The Freud Museum, London 7; Hulton Deutsch 45, 70; JS Library International 42; The Kobal Collection 43; The Mansell Collection 47; Rex Features 46, 72, back of pack; Spacecharts 52, 53; Tony Stone Images 55 (Penny Gentieu), 61 (Bruce Ayres), 94; Zefa 8, 19, 21, 40, 59, 64, 66, 84, 86, 87, 89, 90, 92, 95, 96, 97, 99, 100.

The photograph on page 103 is reproduced from Is This Your Day? by George Thommen, Crown, New York, 1973.

Acknowledgements

For their support and encouragement, many thanks to my mother and Ian Moseley, and to Seamus Considine, John Dolby, Stephen Dolby, Dr Keith Jolles, the late Pauline McGill, Christopher Peat, Dr Heinz Tittmar, and helpful friends from Mensa. I should also like to acknowledge help received under the DTI Enterprise Initiative, and from Wharmby Associates. Finally, I should like to record my sincere appreciation for the significant editorial contribution to this book from my editor, Pat Pierce.

Project Editor	Pat Pierce	Assistant Designer	Rachel Kirkland
Proof Readers	Sophie Bevan	Illustrator	Anthony Duke
	and Tessa Monina	Picture Researcher	Liz Eddison
Indexer	Dorothy Frame	Production	Charles James
Art Director	Elaine Partington		and Hazel Kirkman
Art Editor	Sarah Howerd		

Eddison Sadd would like to extend special thanks to Pat Pierce.